Lear Malaysian by association

Lingo Links ™

The easy playful way to learn a new language.

Written by: James Harvey

Published in the UK by James
Harvey 2015

ISBN-13: ISBN-978-1517335380

Learn Malaysian by association –
Lingo Links
First Edition

Dedicated to:

Sri Sumaryani Swarno for all her marvelous support, editing and patience.

Jelila for your example and passion. Without you I never would have started.

Olive Harvey for always being there.

Contents

Forward 1

    A personal note from the Author.............................. 1

Lingo Links™ Language Learning. 2

How and why it works.. 3

    Research Evidence... 5

    Using this book 6

    How to learn a new word. 8

    Your First Words in Malaysian 10

    Notations used 11

    Avoiding confusions 12

    Handling Grammar. 13

A little bit about Malaysia 14

    Overview 14

    Customs 16

Let's get stuck in 18

    Every day vocabulary 18

    How to check you've integrated the words. 20

    Here are a few more words...................................22

    Using the words you've learned so far 25

I , My ,Me - You, Your 26

Let's learn some more words.............................. 28

    Be my guest at the Airport tomorrow 28

    The Cat's in the toilet at the restaurant. 32

Past, present, future 36

Soak up some more vocab 38

    Wake up thirsty without clothes 38

    Hot week to move out the village 41

Some sentence structure 45

Descriptive word order 45

Making Plurals 46

Practice using the words you've learned 47

Get some more vocab 48

Now you're nearly fluent! 48

Don't cook ice cream on your Birthday 52

Greetings - Times of the Day 55

Good morning, afternoon, evening, night & bye 55

Phrases & Slang out and about 58

How's it going? 58

No Problem 59

Colloquial city and sms 60

Sentence practice part 1 63

Some more great words to learn 64

Late for the dance party 64

White sand, weather and sauce 67

More words for your Malaysian journey 70

Sorry for the rain and mosquitoes 70

Yes you can learn many words 73

Rubbish Taxi's and a place to sleep 73

Get ready to start the download 76

Sentence practice part 2 79

Unusual Foods and fruits 80

Never, ever and possessions. 83

How to use ever and never. 83

How to indicate possessions and "the" 84

You can remember so many more... 85

Sit down, have a Coffee 85

Old pancakes and black phones 88

How to say I'm doing that first 91

Chat ups, romance and lovers! 92

Darling, I love your eyes 92

Sentence practice part 3 95

Words on the home straight 96

Is it true your Father smells? 96

Small change for your family under the tree 100

Numbers & Money 103

Learning your numbers and all about money. 103

One to Ten (1 - 10) 104

Eleven to Nineteen (11 - 19) 106

The tens (20, 30, 40....) 107

Hundreds, Thousands and Millions 108

Ordinals and No. of times. 110

Date and Time 112

Months and Days of the week 112

Month names 112

What's the date? 114

Days of the week 115

Seasons 117

Telling the time 118

Time durations 119

Sentence practise part 4 120

Congratulations 121

About the Author 122

Connect with James 123

Coming soon... 123

Answers to sections & quizzes 124

Past, Present, Future practice 124

Numbers check 125

Sentence practice 1 126

Sentence practice 2 127

Sentence practice 3 128

Sentence practice 4 129

Pronunciation **130**

Vowels 130

Consonants: 131

Alphabet 133

Index **134**

Your Notes. **140**

Forward

A personal note from the Author

First and foremost, thanks for buying this book. It's aimed at providing you with a fast, easy and fun way to learn. I hope you find this book as liberating as I have for both learning and for communicating with others in Malaysian. I've made it as playful and uplifting as I can, and sometimes gritty to evoke strong emotions. I am aware it's not the last word on language education, but, my word it's fast and effective.

Speaking other languages requires courage especially for those of us who have been put down in our learning. The best way I know of overcoming this is to be gentle with yourself. You'll gain confidence from having this memory technique at your disposal as the words you need just bubble up so you don't have to struggle. Remember, the majority of people will be grateful that you are doing your best to speak their language and will support you.

Travel is an expanding experience. When you have a local language that experience becomes far richer.

I'd love to hear from you, your comments and feedback, so please drop me a line. You'll find my contact details at the end of the book and you can sign up for updates on my website.

With love, James

Lingo Links™ Language Learning
www.lingolinks.biz

𝓛𝓲𝓷𝓰𝓸 𝓛𝓲𝓷𝓴𝓼™ 𝓛𝓪𝓷𝓰𝓾𝓪𝓰𝓮 𝓛𝓮𝓪𝓻𝓷𝓲𝓷𝓰.

Learn Malaysian fast with this amazing memory technique. It's easy, engaging and long-lasting, no more book worming with boring lists of words – **Lingo Links™** sets you free to learn in your own way and at your own pace, with great results. You already know a language so why not use it to add new words onto what you already know. Using this method, you can learn hundreds of words remarkably quickly and easily.

Get Wise!

Lingo Links™ works by creating associations from the English words you already know, to the new words you want to learn. The more outrageous or funny the association, the easier it is to remember. The more vivid your experiences, the more you remember about them, right!

Hi from James

As an instructor in Laughter Yoga, Improvised Comedy and Creative Dance, I love using humour and word play to learn and have fun. I originally learned Indonesian using this method and have adapted it to learn and teach Malaysian. I started learning with a course going through a workbook twice a week for a month. It was so dry and such a struggle to learn the words, I thought "I'll never manage this!" Then I remembered a technique I'd come across and started to use it to learn Malaysian.

It's a memory technique that I've augmented with my own methods to make it more effective. It totally turned around my belief that I couldn't learn a new language – what I found was – I just didn't know how to have fun doing so! That's what I want to share with you, fun effective learning.

Lingo Links™ Language Learning
www.lingolinks.biz

How and why it works

This style of learning is three times more effective than traditional methods. It uses a consequence of how your brain works, (that is little known), to record new words in your memory, quickly and effectively.

"*I expect you all to be independent, innovative, critical thinkers who will do exactly as I say!*"

The left side of your brain is primarily involved with logic and language (unless you are left handed). This hemisphere on its own can learn new words, but it's a bit like trying to glue words onto a piece of paper on a windy day - not many stick!

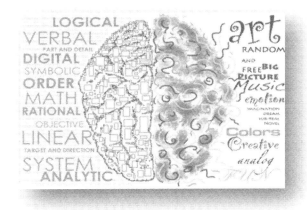

The right side of your brain is involved in emotions, creativity and intuition. This side can imagine, invent and visualise which is great for learning new experiences, but doesn't do language. So guess what...

When you bring these two parts together, magic happens. By getting emotionally involved and imagining or visualising *(more on how to do that later)*, you create strong experiences which stimulate learning. When you use this with another brain trick, called hooking, you remember new words very easily.

Hooking is where we already have an idea or thing remembered and we hook (or link on) something else on to it. For example, if you already have a basis in using a computer, it's easier to learn how to use a smart phone. It's the same with art or any skill.

Here you simply use the English words you already know to hook on new Malaysian words which is highly effectively.

Research Evidence

Studies carried out by Atkinson & Raugh show a marked improvement in retention of language using a word association or a mnemonic method of learning.

The experiments compared learning using, what they called, a keyword method of learning, versus a control group, who used traditional methods of learning such as repetition and by rote.

Participants were given an English keyword that sounded like the foreign word they were learning, and then a mental image of that keyword, essentially an association. The results when learning Spanish were remarkable.

- **88% of the words were retained using the method**
- **28% of the words retained learning by rote**

For learning Spanish – the results were **over 3 times better** than learning using traditional methods.

The same research team also found that retention significantly improved. They found people achieved:

- **50% Better immediate recall**
- **75% Improvement longer term**

And this was learning Russian, which is far more difficult to associate than Malaysian.

"I found this research subsequent to learning Malaysian with this method. Personally, my retention and long term recall has been remarkable, but of course, I can't prove it to you. The best thing is to try it for yourself" – James.

Let's see how to use this book to support you most effectively...

Using this book

This book is about learning Malaysian vocabulary and simple grammar so you can speak and write Malaysian. It presents lists of simple everyday words along with associations and visualisations which activate your memory for learning. You read an association for a word, close your eyes and imagine, visualise or experience the scene or situation in your mind. An incredible number of words can be learned quickly and permanently in a short time using this simple method.

Free your Mind...

If you find visualising difficult (actually seeing something in your mind's eye), then simply get the feeling of the sentence, hear the words in your head as if you are experiencing, sensing or hearing it happen in front of you, and/or imagine yourself acting it out.

Each of us has a primary method of learning – Visual (pictures - images), Auditory (listening - words) and Kinaesthetic (more physical – solid). Most people are Visual these days due to the influences of media, Television etc. I've found the best thing you can do is to "Play" with each way and see what works best for YOU, you might be surprised! The more you practice, the easier and quicker it gets. You become more proficient the more you learn – how many other language techniques make you more effective the more you learn!

Now you can relax - I have done all the hard work for you and made the associations so you don't have to. Let your imagination fly – the more richly you can experience the association, the stronger the memory of the words you will have.

The associations may not present an exact pronunciation of the word you are learning. Often there is no exact match to hook the new word to and so an approximation is required. This is not as important as you might think. The association will give you the ability to retrieve the word you want from your memory, like a key to a lock, it opens the door. Your mind then presents you with the actual word you want.

I have given pronunciation tips where the association doesn't quite sound like the word you are learning, or it's not obvious from simply reading it.

You'll also find a pronunciation section at the back of the book, but for now, the most important thing is to **roll your R's,** pronounce **C** is **Ch** as in **Chair** and to swallow your **G's** like the first **G in Gang** (*GG is pronounced the same as G in English*). Most other letters are pronounced very close to English, which is a great help for us.

Next, let's look at an example of how to learn a word...

How to learn a new word.

Here's an example of how to learn the word **Good** in Malaysian.

The word for **Good** is **Bagus**.

For each word being learned, the English word, then the Malaysian word is presented. In this case:

Good – Bagus

Next we give a sentence for you to make the association between the two. This works by using words you already know as a hook to the new word you want to learn.

Read the sentence then imagine the scene (visualising, hearing, experiencing as you wish). The more vivid and stronger your experience, the more effective your learning will be.

Try this example below for the word Good.

Good – Bagus

Imagine a **bad goose** that mended its ways and is now going around doing **good** deeds like washing up.

The words underlined are the ones we are associating.

Take your time with the scene. Imagine it happening, seeing it in your mind's eye, hearing the sounds or words, feeling the sensations...

The more colour, texture, and sounds you add the more it will lodge in your memory.

This example works very well as it is fairly ridiculous because Geese never do good deeds and especially washing up! (*At least not the ones that chased me the last time I met them*).

Remember, the more outlandish the idea, the stronger the memory that is created.

Once you've used your imagination to picture, feel or sense the scene, think of the word <u>Good</u> and rehearse the scene in your mind one more time paying particular attention to the association.

That's it! It's now in your memory.

When you want to say a word in Malaysian like **Good**, you will immediately have the picture of a Goose in your mind, or the sensation of it, or the word, and then you'll remember the Goose was a **bad goose** and then you'll have the word for **Good** in Malaysian right there - **Bagus**.

The words I have chosen for associations in the book give you the pronunciation as close as I can find. For example, the **ba** or **bad** and the **goos** of **goose** are exactly how to say the word. In some cases, where it's unclear or difficult to find matching English sounds, I have given pronunciation tips.

After a while, the association disappears *(if you're worried about having errant Geese running around your head)* and you just 'know' the word you need.

Using this method you can learn hundreds of words in a very short space of time. That's all there is to it. It is amazing how effective it is. Recruiting both sides of your brain to learn new words really works.

Let's learn a few words right now...

Your First Words in Malaysian

Hello/Hi - Halo/Hai
It's the same so imagine saying hello to a person
wrapped in a Malaysian flag.

*When words are the same or very similar we use the
Malaysian flag as the association so we remember
it's the same in both Languages. (The flag is red and
white).*

Yes – Ya
Imagine you go to a posh event and everyone there has double
chins and says "yar" instead of yes.

Language – Bahasa
Imagine a Sheep that can't Baa,
has a definite Language problem.

The next few pages cover notations used, how *not grouping*
words by category aids learning, how we cover grammar in the
book and a little bit about Malaysia.

You can skip these if you like and start right now by jumping to
the chapter Let's get stuck in.

Notations used

The book uses some short hand notations to help with pronunciation and explanations.

The following are used throughout the book:

(Pr: xxxxxx)

When you see (Pr: xxxxxx) this means that the xxxxxx is a word or sound to help you with the pronunciation of the word you are learning.

(Lit: xxxxx xxxx)

When you see (Lit: xxxxx xxxx) this means that the xxxx xxxx is a literal translation of the sentence or word preceding it.

The literal translation will help to make the sentence structure more obvious for you, as the word order or the way words are used, are not always the same is in English.

Avoiding confusions

When learning new words, there is a temptation to learn associated words at the same time, e.g. Good Morning, Afternoon, Evening and Good Night, colours, directions and so on. Also, to learn opposites, hot and cold, good and bad...

When we learn related words at the same time, our brain finds it harder to remember which of the choices is the one we need. This is also true for any Malaysian words we are learning that look or sound similar.

For this reason, I have done my best to keep similar related words and Malaysian words that look or sound similar, separate. This makes it much easier to retain and re-produce the right word for any situation. That's why the book is not divided up into, categories like **Greetings**, **At the Restaurant** and so on like other language learning and phrase books. It just doesn't work very well for us to learn related words at the same time. It is a useful structure for a phrase book, however, this book is primarily about learning vocabulary so that you don't need one!

Not all words lend themselves to be learned separately. For example, numbers, dates and times are best presented together so I've given them their own sections. On the whole, learning associated words separately is far more effective.

Helpful Tips

With opposites, you can give yourself a leg up by learning one side of the opposite and then the word for <u>not</u>. This way you can double the number of expressions you have really fast!

Handling Grammar.

Having an extensive vocabulary to draw on in a language is an amazing help, but there are some rules to languages to get the words in the right order *and* certain modifiers that change verbs.

Fortunately, in Malaysian, there are very few modifiers for tenses. What happened in the past, what's happening now or what's going to happen in the future are mostly handled by context. Also, in general for spoken Malaysian, any verb modifiers there are, are mostly dropped. This is great news for us.

Some of the word order is not the same as in English, so I have added sections in the book to help you out. This will help you get the word order more correct.

The aim of this book, as in any communication, is to be understood, and most of the time, even if the word order is mixed up, you'll get the message across. If not, Malaysians are amazing helpful at correcting you.

I have interspersed the sections for tenses, word order and other items (such as slang & colloquialisms) throughout the book as a learning aid and to keep you stimulated. Malaysian is a much more simple language than English, but we still need to know how to understand and map that simplicity.

The next section is a little background about Malaysia – but if you want to dive straight into learning words – go ahead and skip it.

A little bit about Malaysia

Overview

Malaysia (*a combination of the word "Malay" and the Latin-Greek suffix "-sia"*) consists of thirteen states and three federal territories and, having a variety of languages and dialects, uses the official Language Bahasa Melayu (Malay Language) to communicate.

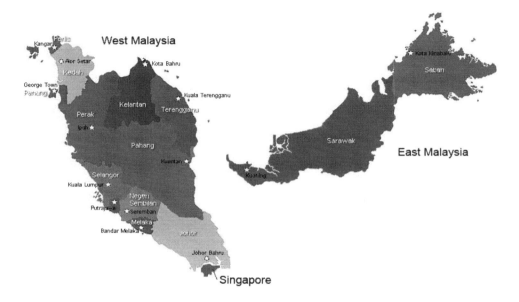

Malaysian is thought to have originated in Borneo and spoken by over 28 million people in Malaysia. It is also one of the four official languages of Singapore and can also be used (with a few word exceptions) in Indonesia covering a massive 270 million speakers worldwide.

Malaysian was established as the official language of Malaysia in 1967 and widely adopted in 1969 after the Race Riots. It uses many words borrowed from Arabic (mainly religious terms), Sanskrit, Tamil, Persian, Portuguese, Dutch, certain Chinese dialects and more recently, English (in particular many scientific and technological terms). You will also find "Manglish", a combination of English and Malay which is a colloquial form of English with heavy Malay, Chinese, and Tamil influences.

Malaysian is compulsory in official correspondence, legal documents etc. particularly in the government. If you are travelling in Malaysia, it's the best language to learn as you'll be able to communicate with the most number of people and find your way around.

Besides language, there are some cultural considerations that you might find useful to take into account when communicating. Communication isn't just about the words, it's also about understanding and relating to the person you are talking to.

Several of the Malaysian customs may seem strange to you, but to avoid causing offence it is good to know a few things about the background of Malaysia and some do's and don'ts.

Customs

The population of Malaysia consists of many ethnic groups, mostly from local regions, however around 25% are of Chinese decent and 7% Indian.

The primary religion of Malaysia is Muslim, however, most religions are represented across Malaysia; Buddhist, Christian and Taoist amongst them with the majority of the Indian population being Hindu.

When meeting someone for the first time you can often shake hands, however, wait to see if their hand is offered first because some will only shake hands with another Muslim. If this is the case, a friendly good day will suffice.

They may shake hands in a different way from you by offering their right hand while their left lightly touches their own wrist. Then their right hand touches their own chest to show they are sincerely pleased to have met you.

If a Malay hands anything to you, they will often do it in the same way that they shake hands. That is, the thing they are giving you is held in his right hand while the left hand touches the right wrist. Malays never give you anything with their left hand. This is considered very rude indeed.

A man does not display affection for a woman in public. Although it does not seem to be frowned on for Westerners to do it, you may cause offence if you publically display affection for a Malaysian of the opposite sex. This is not such an issue in the big cities, more in rural areas.

Lingo Links™ Language Learning
www.lingolinks.biz

In polite company, either when sitting on the floor or on chairs, Malays do not point their feet at anyone else. This too is thought to be bad mannered. Just avoid it in general!

Malays, Chinese and Indians all strive to maintain face and avoid shame both in public and private. Openly criticising, putting down, insulting or generally putting someone on the spot should be avoided. Remaining calm and courteous; discussing errors or transgressions in private; speaking about problems without blaming anyone and using non-verbal communication to say "no" will all help to maintain face. *Be aware Malaysians find it very hard to say "no", so, maybe will mostly mean "no - but I don't want to offend you"!*

Most people are not punctual – relax – you're in Malaysia!

These are a few pointers to help you on your way. Generally, I have found the Malaysians to be pretty tolerant, but I also like to promote respect for their customs, and hope you do too.

This chart of Malaysia shows how diverse the people are.

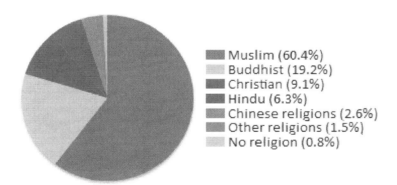

Muslim (60.4%)
Buddhist (19.2%)
Christian (9.1%)
Hindu (6.3%)
Chinese religions (2.6%)
Other religions (1.5%)
No religion (0.8%)

Distribution of Malaysian Religions.

Let's get stuck in

Every day vocabulary

Here are some words that will allow you to have some basic conversation extremely quickly. Later in the section you can check your learning and see some examples of how to use the words you have learned.

Above all – HAVE FUN!!!

Remember – the more vivid you make the association, the stronger the memory of each word will be.

Thank you - Terima kasih
Imagine you tear the seat of your taxi's car as you get out and he says "Thank you for tearing my car seat"

I – Saya
Imagine you meet a man who sighs a lot and introduces himself as, "It is I the sigher".

Name – Nama (Pr: Num er)
Imagine trying to name a famous person!

To – Ke (Pr: Ke as in Kerb)
Imagine going to your car and you get interrupted and only get as far as saying the C of the word car!

No/Not -Tidak
Imagine you are bird watching and your friend asks you "Is that the rare tea drinking duck?" you reply "No, it's not the Tea Duck, it's a Bali duck!".

Please/Help – Tolong (Used as in "Help me to...")
Imagine when you break down you ask "<u>please</u> I'd need a <u>tow</u> a<u>long</u> the road to get me home".

How are you - Apa khabar (Pr: Ah Pa Ka Bar)
Imagine a magician asking <u>how are you</u> and waving his wand with an <u>abra kadabra</u>.

Understand - Faham
Imagine you can't <u>understand</u> why you can hear a <u>far</u> off <u>hum</u> in your ears.

Price – Harga (nya) *(The suffix nya turns Price into The price)*
Imagine you are buying something and you must bargain <u>harder</u> for a good <u>price</u>, you can't get it so you say '<u>nya</u>' I don't want it!

Go – Pergi
Imagine you have a cat called Gi and wherever you <u>go</u> makes it Purr! <u>Purr Gi.</u>

How to check you've integrated the words.

This section helps you to find out which words you've remembered and which you need to review. This is a really important part of the book because the more you practice using the association to recall the words, the stronger your memory of them will be.

From the list presented below, first cover the Malaysian column and say the word you have just learned out loud. Then cover the English column and translate the Malaysian words out loud. This helps you to translate in both directions. If you only translate one way, you may find that you can speak Malaysian, but not understand it!

The words in the practise list are intentionally not in the original order. We tend to remember things at the beginning and end of lists, so mixing up the order will help you remember more effectively.

For any words that you don't fully remember, go back over the association and do the check again. Sometimes it takes a couple of goes to cement the word in your memory.

Once you've completed a list, congratulate yourself on what you have achieved and avoid putting yourself down for what you didn't remember. Positive reinforcement works and will encourage you to perform better and better.

If you are interested in writing in Malaysian – write the words down as well as saying them to check you have the spelling accurate.

Here's your first practice list to check the words you've learned so far...

Lingo Links™ Language Learning
www.lingolinks.biz

Checking what you've learned

English	Malaysian
Name	Nama
Please/Help	Tolong
No/Not	Tidak
To	Ke
How are you?	Apa Khabar?
Thank you	Terima kasih
Understand	Faham
Price	Harga(nya)
Go	Pergi
I	Saya

Remember – go back over any that you haven't remembered yet and congratulate yourself for those you have. Positive reinforcement works.

Revisiting the practice, recalling the associations, helps to cement the words in your memory.

Here are a few more words...

Where – Di Mana *(Where something is)*
Imagine looking on a map to find <u>where</u> a huge manor house built in the shape of the letter D. <u>Where</u> is that <u>D manor</u>?

You – Awak (Pr: Ah wack)
Imagine you meet yourself in a dream and don't know if <u>you</u> are <u>awake</u> or asleep!

How – Bagaimana (Pr: bag eye ma na)
Imagine <u>how</u> hard it is to <u>bag</u> an <u>Iguana</u>.

Remember – the associations may not present an exact pronunciation of the word you are learning but will give your brain the key to retrieve the actual word(s) far more effectively.

OK / Fine – Baik (most used in response to 'how are you'?)

Imagine it's <u>OK</u> to ride your new <u>bike</u> with a frame made from the letters, <u>OK.</u>

Want – Mahu
Imagine a child that says M instead of N saying, it's mine and I <u>want</u> it <u>mow</u>.

Book – Buku
Imagine you are surprised to find your <u>book</u>, there's my <u>book</u> <u>Ooo</u>.

Finish(ed) - Selesai (doing something)
Imagine being a salesman who knows you are <u>finished</u> learning about sales when you can <u>sell a sigh</u>.

Who - Siapa
Imagine thinking, I wonder <u>who</u> that is with the pipe and slippers. You <u>see a Pa</u>, that's who.

How much/many – Berapa banyak
Imagine you are in Tibet and want to know <u>how much</u> the Yaks are but you can't find out <u>how many</u> there are because the <u>bear-rapper</u>s have <u>ban</u>ned <u>Yak</u>s on their tour.

Stay (live) - Tinggal
Imagine you feel a <u>tingle</u> when you <u>stay</u> in Malaysia.

That – Itu
Imagine you are shopping so insistently that you'll have <u>that</u> hat and take <u>it too</u>!

Can – Boleh
Imagine seeing a magic trick with a bowl and asking the magician, "<u>can</u> I look at the <u>bowl eh</u>!"

Checking what you've learned

English	Malaysian
How	Bagaimana
That	Itu
Finished	Selesai
Can	Boleh
Who	Siapa
How much/many	Berapa banyak
You	Awak
OK	Baik
Where (is)	Di Mana
Book	Buku
Want	Mahu
Stay	Tinggal

Please congratulate yourself for what you remembered and go back over any that haven't quite landed.

If reviewing feels like a chore, leave it until later. Keeping learning light encourages you to come back and do more 'cause it's fun.

Go easy on yourself, the more you appreciate your accomplishments (rather than berate your failures), the happier you are to learn more.

Using the words you've learned so far

There's lots of things you can say even with the few words you've learned so far. It's amazing how quickly you can communicate so much with so little effort.

Here are some examples of using the words you've seen so far.

I've added the literal translation of the words so you can get an idea of some word order (which we will cover later) and for a flavour of the language usage.

Phrase	Translation	Literally
Hello, how are you?	Hai, apa khabar?	Hi, what news?
Fine, thanks!	Baik, terima kasih!	OK/fine thank you
What's your name?	Siapa nama awak?	Who name you?
My name's John	Nama saya John	Name I John
I would like that	Saya mahu itu	I want that
How much is that?	Berapa harganya?	How many (price) is that?
I don't understand	Saya tidak faham	I no/not understand
Where do you live?	Di mana awak tinggal?	Where you stay/live?
Are you finished?	Awak selesai?	You finished?
I want to go to...	Saya mahu pergi ke...	I want go to...

Even with these few words at your disposal you can greet people, ask their name and give them yours, ask how much something is, ask to go somewhere and say if you understand or not - just in a few minutes.

1 , My ,Me - You, Your

Malaysian is far simpler than English. When you want to talk about yourself, **(I, me)**, or refer to anything you possess **(my)** or someone else and what they possess **(you, your)** it's a breeze. There are only two words to consider, **Saya & Awak**. It's where they are used in a sentence gives them their meaning.

Here's a handy table for quick reference.

English	Malaysian	Use
I	Saya	Before
My	Saya	After
Me	Saya	After
You	Awak	Before & After
Your	Awak	After

Let's look at this in practice...

Use of Saya

At the beginning of a sentence **Saya** means I and at the end it means **my** or **me**.

> **"I want that"** is **"Saya mahu itu"** (Lit: I want that)
>
> **"My Book"** is **"Buku saya"** (Lit: Book I)
>
> **"Please understand me"** is **"Tolong fahami saya"**

Use of Awak

At the beginning of a sentence **Awak** means **You** and at the end it means **Your**.

"**Do you want that**" is "**Awak mahu itu**"

"**Your Book**"   is "**Buku awak**"   (Lit: Book you)

"**Where are you?**"   is "**Di mana awak?**" (Lit: Where you?)

In the last two cases, **Awak** goes in the same place in a sentence as in English.

Let's learn some more words

Be my guest at the Airport tomorrow

Rice - Nasi
Imagine you take your friend to see how <u>rice</u> grows, they think it grows on trees, and you show them a plant and say '<u>na see</u>, rice grows from the ground'.

Will – Akan
Imagine you are at an airfield and you <u>will</u> learn to fly, then you can tell everyone "<u>I can</u>".

Learn/Study – Belajar
Imagine you are <u>learning</u> chemistry and you need to use a huge <u>bell jar</u> to contain all your notes.

Be my guest,
Go ahead or Please – Silakan
(When you are offering something)
Imagine you offer a can of drink to your friend and say, <u>go ahead</u>, <u>be my guest</u> try open this <u>silly can.</u>

Airport - Bandara
Imagine you get stopped by security for wearing a <u>Bawakna</u> into the <u>Airport</u>!

House – Rumah
Imagine an Italian comes round your house and remarks – ah, nice <u>Rooma'</u> in your <u>house</u>!

Car – Kereta
Imagine you feel really lucky you managed to swerve your new <u>car</u> around a huge <u>crater</u> in the road.

Beach - Pantai.
Imagine you go to the <u>beach</u> and everyone has a pan around their necks. You ask someone and they explain it's the new fashion beach wear called a <u>Pan Tie</u>.

Water – Air (Pr: Eyer)
Imagine you now drop your H's as you lift some <u>water</u> '<u>igher</u> and 'igher.

Know - Tahu (Pr: Tow as in Towel or as Ta Who)
Imagine a friend denies taking your Towel from the bathroom, but you <u>know</u> that '<u>tow</u>el' is yours.

Tomorrow – Esok
Imagine <u>tomorrow</u> you go to the cleaners to wash your best socks but you only take one b<u>est</u> <u>sock</u> at a time!

There is/are – Ada *(Like have)*
Imagine <u>there is</u> an <u>Adder</u> in the grass in your garden, you turn around and suddenly <u>there are</u> Adders everywhere!

Problem - Masalah
Imagine you are in an Indian restaurant – call the waiter over and tell them there's a <u>problem</u> with your chicken '<u>Masala'.</u>

Swimming – Renang
Imagine you want to go for a <u>swim</u> but they <u>rename</u> your favourite <u>swimming</u> pool so you can't find it.

Already – Sudah
Imagine your friend telling you all about Sue and her bad habit of picking her nose. You say, "But I <u>already</u> met <u>Sue, da</u>!"

Lingo Links™ Language Learning
www.lingolinks.biz

Brown – Coklat
Imagine you trod in something <u>brown</u> and your relief when you realise that you just trod on bar of <u>chocolate</u>.

Where – Ke mana (As in *"to go"* – *Pr: Ke as in Kerb*)
Imagine <u>where</u> you desperately want to go is the new apple <u>c</u>ore <u>manor</u>.

Checking what you've learned

English	Malaysian
Will	Akan
Be my guest/If you please	Silakan
Swimming	Renang
Car	Kereta
Airport	Bandara
Rice	Nasi
Brown	Coklat
Tomorrow	Esok
House	Rumah
Problem	Masalah
Learn	Belajar
Already	Sudah
Beach	Pantai
Where (to go)	Ke mana
Know	Tahu
Water	Air
There is/are	Ada

Remember you can go back over any that haven't quite landed.

The Cat's in the toilet at the restaurant.

Coconut - Kelapa
Imagine a dog drinking keys from a <u>coconut</u> shell. That dogs a <u>key lapper</u>.

Sugar - Gula
Imagine your French friend telling you he spilt some <u>sugar</u>, now there is <u>Goo la</u> (Goo there).

Cat – Kucing (Pr: c as ch in chair)
Imagine a <u>Cat</u> stuck in a till. You open the till and it makes the sound, <u>ke-ching</u>!

There – Di sana
Imagine you are camping and need to go the toilet block all the way over <u>there</u> to <u>De-Sana</u>tise the toilet.

Toilet - Tandas
Imagine a you leave your <u>toilet</u> out in the sun and it gets as <u>tanned</u> <u>as</u> a Brazilian model.

Later – Nanti
Imagine you are excited that <u>later</u> you will go to your Nan's for Tea and have <u>Nan-Tea.</u>

Restaurant – Restoran
Imagine you enter a <u>Restaurant</u> and they have no tea so it's a <u>Restauran</u>!

Big - Besar
Imagine you get really lost in a really <u>big</u> Turkish <u>bazaar</u>.

When - Bila
Imagine you are so happy <u>when</u> you find a café where you can have a coffee and they send your <u>bill a</u> day later.

Tea – Teh (Pr: Tai as in Tail)
Imagine a <u>tea</u> cup with the handle shaped like the letter 'a'. Now break off the handle and you have a cup of <u>Te</u>.

Red – Merah
Imagine you are <u>red</u> from sun burn at a horse trial where there are so many horses you can see a <u>mare a</u> minute.

Drink - Minum
Imagine you are in a coffee shop and you order the <u>minimum</u> size <u>drink</u>.

Yesterday – Semalam
Imagine you took your pet sheep out <u>yesterday</u> and a man asked you what is was, you said, "<u>Sir</u>, that's <u>m'lamb</u>".

Eat - Makan
Imagine you <u>make an</u> omelette to <u>eat</u> which is the most delicious thing you ever ate.

Motor Bike – Motosikal
Imagine that you are out on your <u>Motor Bike</u> and an old <u>Motorcycle</u> zooms past you.

Without - Tanpa
Imagine that <u>without</u> sun cream you will get your Father brown, now you can <u>Tan Pa</u>. (Pa as is Papa)

Buy - Beli
Imagine you go to an amazing store to <u>buy</u> some shoes and you cannot <u>beli</u>eve how cheap they are.

Now – Sekarang
Imagine you telephone someone they ask you what you are doing <u>now</u>, and you say, this <u>sec' I rang</u>?

Checking what you've learned

English	Malaysian
Sugar	Gula
There	Di sana
Restaurant	Restoran
Eat	Makan
Toilet	Tandas
Coconut	Kelapa
Red	Merah
Later	Nanti
Without	Tanpa
Now	Sekarang
Yesterday	Semalam
Cat	Kucing
Tea	Teh
Big	Besar
When	Bila
Drink	Minum
Buy	Beli
Motorbike	Motosikal

Remember – go back over any that you haven't remembered yet and congratulate yourself for those your have.

Positive reinforcement works!

Past, present, future

In Malaysian the concept of past, present or future is not given by the verb changing as it is in English, but from using other words that give context to the time frame.

Things in Malaysian either have happened, are happening now, or will happen.

Past - Happened

To indicate something in the past, we use the word **Sudah (Already)**. It has *already* happened.

For example:

'Have you eaten?' is phrased as **'You already eat?'**

Awak sudah makan?

This phrase is used often in Malaysia as they are very keen on knowing whether you have eaten or not as they like to look after family, and you are part of theirs.

Present - Now

To indicate something is happening now we can emphasise by saying it is in the process of happening, (although the present is usually implied). For that we need the word "Sedang".

In the process of – Sedang
Imagine you are <u>in the process of</u> listening to what an online lecturer <u>said</u> while you <u>hang</u> your clothes our in the garden.

For example:

'Are you eating?' is phrased as **'You in the process eat?'**

Awak sedang makan?

Future – Will happen

To indicate something is going to happen in the future we use the word **Akan** – **Will**. This *will* happen.

'I'm going to eat' is phrased as **'I will eat'**

Saya akan makan.

Using date and time references

You can use a date or time to relate something in the future or past, like **Tomorrow (Esok)** or **Yesterday (Semalam)**. This again greatly simplifies the structure of the language and reduces the number of words you need to say.

For example:
'I'm going to the airport tomorrow'
Esok saya pergi ke bandara (Lit: I go to Airport tomorrow)

'I went to the beach yesterday'
Saya pergi ke pantai semalam (Lit: I go to beach yesterday)

Quiz: Translate these for fun!

- I will go to the beach
- I've been swimming
- I will eat later
- I went to the Airport yesterday
- Saya mahu pergi ke Bandara esok
- Awak sudah makan?
- Esok kamu akan pergi?

Answers to quizzes are in the back of the book.

Lingo Links™ Language Learning
www.lingolinks.biz

Soak up some more vocab

Wake up thirsty without clothes

Thirsty – Haus
Imagine the roof leaks in your <u>house</u> because it is <u>thirsty</u>.

Hair - Rambut
Imagine you're getting your hair cut near a farm and an angry <u>Ram butt</u> you on your <u>hair.</u>

Return - Pulang
Imagine you are excited to <u>return</u> home to work on your new invention to hang pulleys – called the <u>Pull hang.</u>

Bottle – Botol
Imagine you want a <u>bottle</u> with a bow on it, only you're upset because in this country there's a <u>bow toll!</u>

Knife - Pisau
Imagine someone pokes you with a <u>knife</u> while you're taking a piss – you hear <u>piss – Ow</u>!

Half – Separuh
Imagine you go to a hotel and only pay <u>half</u> because you didn't take <u>separate</u> <u>rooms</u>.

Alone - Sendiri
Imagine when you are <u>alone</u>, you write in your naughty thoughts in your <u>sin diary</u>.

Fork - Garpu
Imagine your new job is to pick up <u>Garfield's</u> <u>poo</u> with a <u>fork</u>!

Wake up - Bangun
Imagine you <u>wake up</u> when you hear the
<u>bang</u> of a <u>gun</u>.

More – Lebih
Imagine your frustration with the
government. The <u>more</u> you try to avoid
tax, the more they <u>levy</u> on you.

Skirt - Skirt
Imagine you are wearing a <u>skirt</u> with a Malaysian
flag pattern on it.

Clothes - Pakaian
Imagine you are packing a suit case of <u>clothes</u> and you pack your
friend Ian by mistake. With your clothes, you <u>pack a Ian</u>.

Give – Beri
Imagine you have to <u>bury</u> all the presents you want <u>give</u> to your
new Dog, because he hates wrapping paper.

Pen – Pena
Imagine an Italian asking for a pen, he says "I want a pen'a".

Take – Ambil
Imagine that you feel so rich that you <u>amble</u> over to the cashier
to <u>take</u> your pay check.

Bring – Bawa
Imagine you need training how to bow to the King so he asks to
<u>bring</u> the professional <u>bower</u> to show you how it's done.

Vegetable – Sayur
Imagine you're a famous <u>vegetable</u> producer and your fans want
you to <u>sign</u> <u>your</u> name on their vegetables.

They – Mereka
Imagine watching your friends in amazement as <u>they</u> play one
Spanish <u>maraca</u>.

Lingo Links™ Language Learning
www.lingolinks.biz

Checking what you've learned

English	Malaysian
Take	Ambil
Clothes	Pakaian
Wake up	Bangun
Bottle	Botol
Knife	Pisau
Vegetable	Sayur
Alone	Sendiri
Pen	Pena
Bring	Bawa
Return	Pulang
Give	Beri
Hair	Rambut
They	Mereka
More	Lebih
Fork	Garpu
Thirsty	Haus
Skirt	Skirt
Half	Separuh

Well done, you're amazing!

Remember it's helpful to go back over any that haven't quite landed as long as you're feeling energised.

Lingo Links™ Language Learning
www.lingolinks.biz

Hot week to move out the village

It's remarkable – even by this stage you have learned a massive **Eighty words!**

After this section we will look at some sentence structure and then review some of the words we've learned so you can see how easy it is to make your own sentences...

For now, here are a few more words...

Move out/in – Pindah (*Also used for move in*)
Imagine you 'pinned a' note on the door to let people know you will move out/in!

Still – Masih
Imagine the Superman film is still on at the cinema and you just mus(t) see it

Fruit – Buah-(buahan). (*Say twice and add 'an' for plural*)
Imagine you are throwing fruit at a criminal in the stocks and the crowd ask you to be the town booer.

Then/Later – Kemudian.
Imagine later on telling your friend Ian, if you want to stay happy, then you must get out of that crazy mood Ian.

Village – Kampung
Imagine you go camping in your local village for the night.

Blue – Biru
Imagine using a magic Biro that writes blue letters in the air.

If – Jika
Imagine hiring a car by letter code and if you had the money, you'd get the G-car.

Hot – Panas
Imagine you have got so much food for the barbeque you need a pan as big as the sun to get the food hot.

Expense - Belanja
Imagine making an expense claim for
a <u>Bell</u> <u>and</u> <u>Jar</u> you bought.

Market - Pasar
Imagine going to the <u>Market</u> and get
great deals and you are desperate to
tell a <u>passer</u>-by.

Same - Sama (*Curiously, Sama sama means - Together*)
Imagine you are building a boat and you pass <u>Sam a</u> hammer
which looks the <u>same</u> as a Sharks head.

Also - Juga
Imagine Lady Ga Ga has become Jewish, now she will <u>also</u> be
known as Lady <u>Jew Ga</u>.

Doctor - Doktor
Imagine a Doctor examining you wearing a Malaysian
flag t-shirt!

Week - Minggu
Imagine the terrible <u>week</u> that you got your priceless <u>Ming</u> vase
covered in <u>goo</u>.

Many - Banyak
Imagine <u>many</u> Tibetans get together shouting to <u>ban Yaks</u> in their
country.

Million - Juta
Imagine a Jew giving you a <u>million</u> dollars, and you thank them
appropriately saying, "<u>Jew ta</u>".

Young - Muda
Imagine you are an Italian and upset after someone took your
<u>young</u> girlfriend. Say in an Italian accent "I'm in a <u>mooda</u>!"

Class - Kelas

Imagine going to a Malaysian language class where everything is painted red and white.

Checking what you're learned

English	Malaysian
Then/Later	Kemudian
Village	Kampung
Move out	Pindah
Expense	Belanja
Blue	Biru
Class	Kelas
Still	Masih
Doctor	Doktor
If	Jika
Week	Minggu
Million	Juta
Hot	Panas
Also	Juga
Same	Sama
Fruit	Buah
Market	Pasar
Many	Banyak
Young	Muda

Well done – Woo Hoo!!!

Remember to congratulate yourself for what you remembered and if it feels easy, revisit those you didn't quite get.

Lingo Links™ Language Learning
www.lingolinks.biz

Some sentence structure

Descriptive word order

Sentence structure is pretty easy in Malaysian, but it is different to English. The main difference is where you put the word to describe something.

For example in English we would say   - "The blue car"

In Malaysian you say "Kereta biru"   - "Car blue"

So the descriptive word (adjective) comes after the thing we are talking about (Object / Noun).

<Object / Noun>   <Adjective>

E.g.

   Where is the big house   = Di mana rumah yang besar itu?

   I want to go to the white beach = Saya mahu pergi ke pantai putih

Try these for yourself *(Cover the answers below for now)*

I want red rice...

I want the big brown car....

I want red rice   = Saya mahu nasi merah

I want the big brown car   = Saya mahu kereta besar yang cokelat

Remember, the descriptive word comes after the thing you are talking about.

Lingo Links™ Language Learning
www.lingolinks.biz

Making Plurals

In English we make a plural most commonly by putting **"s"** on the end of a word e.g. **egg -> eggs**, **book -> books**.

Unlike other languages, plurals in Malaysian are very simple. You only need to repeat the noun **(e.g. buku = buku-buku)**, or adding quantitative indicators **(e.g. many, few, number of etc.)** into the sentence.

Most often, Malaysians will imply the plural by the context and not bother to change the word (noun) at all.

For example:

Buku-buku saya = **My books**

Banyak buku = **Lots of books** *(Lit: Many books)*

Mereka kucing awak? = **Are they your cats?**

Practice using the words you've learned

If you've been following the flow of the book, you'll have Ninety nine words at your disposal already. It's amazing what you can say with just this many words.

We also know to put the descriptive word, (adjective), after the thing we are talking about, (noun) and how to make plurals.

Use the following to practice your translations. Cover over the Malaysian answers and translate into Malaysian and then vice-versa to practice in both directions.

Phrase	Translation	Literal meaning
I'm thirsty	Saya haus	I thirst
I want some water	Saya mahu air	I want water
Where's the toilet?	Di mana tandas?	Where toilet
No sugar please	Tolong tanpa gula	Please without sugar
I want to go to the airport	Saya mahu pergi ke bandara	I want go to airport
Where is the market	Di mana pasar	Where market
I don't want this/that	Saya tidak mahu ini/itu	I not want this/that
Red rice please	Tolong nasi merah	Please rice red
I'm learning Malaysian	Saya belajar bahasa Malaysia	I learn language Malaysian
It was hot at the beach yesterday	Itu panas di pantai semalam	That hot at beach yesterday

Get some more vocab

Now you're nearly fluent!

Meat – Daging
Imagine you are vegetarian who's cracked and you're <u>gagging</u> for some <u>meat.</u>

Vegetarian – Vegetarian
The word is the same as it is in English as this concept didn't exist at the time the language was introduced. *You can also say "Tidak daging" (Not meat)*

Isn't it - Kan *(add to the end of a statement to make a question)*
Imagine asking the barmaid in your local bar, "that's a <u>can</u> your holding, <u>isn't it</u>?"

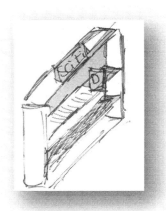

Not – Bukan *(Unlike Tidak, Bukan negates the whole sentence)*
Imagine you're in a library and it's <u>not</u> good because the Star Trek <u>book</u> <u>can</u> not go in the Drama section.

Sit – Duduk (Pr: Do Dook)
Imagine you have very low ceilings in your dining room. Your friend arrives for dinner and you request they d<u>o duck</u> to <u>sit down</u>!

Word - Perkataan
Imagine you ask you Italian friend for a <u>word</u> and she says <u>Purr</u> like a <u>cat</u> 'a c<u>an</u>.

Plate – Pinggan
Imagine you drop a tough <u>plate</u> and as hit hits the floor it goes <u>ping an</u>d rolls away.

Spoon – Sudu
Imagine you are in a posh restaurant with your friend Su and you say to your friend, "<u>Su, do</u> bring a <u>spoon</u> with you when you come back to the table".

Glass (of water) – Gelas
Imagine seeing a rather butch girl in a bar with a glass of <u>water</u> and you remark to your friend, that's a <u>gay-lass</u>! (I know it's not politically correct, it's supposed to evoke emotion so you remember it!)

Plastic – Plastik
Imagine a plastic bag with a Malaysian flag on it! (It's the Malaysian word for a plastic bag and a plastic thing!)

Cold (virus) – Selsema
Imagine you get a <u>cold</u> from working too long outside so you tell your Mum, I've got to <u>sell sema</u>phore flags indoors.

What – Apa *(Also used to turn a statement into a question)*
Imagine you are looking but can't quite make out <u>what</u> is in the rocking chair in your living room – it's your father – <u>Ah Pa</u>!

Bag – Beg
Imagine you have to <u>beg</u> your Mum to buy you're the latest hand <u>bag</u>.

Light/Lamp – Lampu (Room light)
Imagine being nervous to turn on your side table <u>light</u> because it's covered in poo. You know you have a <u>Lamp – poo</u> problem.

Turn (Switch) off – Tutup
Imagine you are an electrician and need <u>to tap</u> the <u>switch</u> to <u>turn</u> it <u>off</u>.

Road – Jalan
Imagine see a Jay bird crossing the <u>road</u> calling out its name Alan. "That's a <u>Jay Alan</u> in the road", you remark.

Stop – Berhenti
Imagine your best friends <u>stop</u> you doing a dare as you are about to drink <u>burnt hen tea</u>.

Bath/Bathe – Mandi
Imagine you're annoyed you have to take a <u>bath</u> with your friend <u>Mandy</u> as she hogs all the soap.

Checking what you've learned

English	Malaysian
Bag	Beg
Not	Bukan
Isn't it	Kan
Meat	Daging
Plate	Pinggan
Sit	Duduk
Bath/Bathe	Mandi
Spoon	Sudu
Vegetarian	Vegetarian
Turn (Switch) Off	Tutup
Glass (of water)	Gelas
Light	Lampu
What	Apa
Road	Jalan
Plastic	Plastik
Word	Perkataan
Cold (virus)	Selsema
Stop	Berhenti

Remember you can back over any that slipped your mind!

Don't cook ice cream on your Birthday

Photo(graph) – foto
Imagine taking a <u>photo</u> of a Malaysian flag!

Year – Tahun (Pr: Ta Hoon)
Imagine every <u>year</u> your love gives you a wonderful silver watch and you say – <u>Ta Hon</u>.

Which – Yang
Imagine helping your spiritual friend trying to decide <u>which</u> they are Yin or <u>Yang</u>.

Very – Sangat
Imagine you are <u>very</u> happy when your friend <u>sang at</u> your birthday party.

Come along (Join) – Ikut
Imagine you are happy when you ask your friend to <u>come along</u> with you to the park and he tells you <u>he could.</u>

Ice Cream – Ais krim (Pr: Ess cream)
Imagine your buy some <u>ice cream</u> and it comes wrapped in a Malaysian flag.

Read – Baca
Imagine going to a wedding as a <u>Bache</u>lor to <u>read</u> your wedding vows.

Birthday – Hari Lahir (Pr: harry la here)
Imagine every <u>birthday</u> your mate <u>Harry</u> wakes you up with singing <u>Lah</u> in your <u>ear</u>.

Pineapple - Nanas
Imagine you go to your <u>Nanas</u> and she gives you a lovely big ripe <u>Pineapple</u>.

Page | **53**

Teacher - Guru
Imagine you are in India to find out about life and your teacher is a Guru.

From - Dari
Imagine you are coming home from a day's work at your organic dairy.

Chair – Kerusi
Imagine sitting in a chair at the beach and a big wave gets you wet so you curse when you see the sea.

Cook - Masak
Imagine you are in a "bring your own food" restaurant and ask the waiter, "I've brought my sack, please will you cook it"?

Salad - Salad
Imagine your salad served on a Malaysian flag!

Massage – Urut (Pr: Ooo root)
Imagine you are feeling tense because tripped over a root in the woods so you decide to you go for a lovely massage.

Don't – Jangan
Imagine you're doing the gardening and you feel lucky you don't own a Jungle an Orchard or a Park.

Feel/Taste – Rasa
Imagine your surprise when you feel you can taste Russia.

Television – Televisyen
Imagine the television is showing a Malaysian flag all day.

Checking what you've learned

English	Malaysian
Photo(graph)	Foto
Salad	Salad
Teacher	Guru
Come along (Join)	Ikut
Very	Sangat
Year	Tahun
Ice Cream	Ais krim
Feel/Taste	Rasa
Which	Yang
Television	Televisyen
Massage	Urut
Read	Baca
Birthday	Hari lahir
Cook	Masak
Pineapple	Nanas
Don't	Jangan
From	Dari
Chair	Kerusi

How did you get on?

Remember to congratulate yourself for what you remembered!

Greetings - Times of the Day

Good morning, afternoon, evening, night & bye

Yes, I'm breaking the rules – but what are rules for??? We're going to learn how to say greetings for times of the day all together.

First, let's introduce "**Selamat**". This wonderful word has many meanings but is basically used to express **happiness** as in the **Good** of **Good Luck** in English. Consequently it's used for the **Good** part of **Good Morning, Afternoon** and so on.

*It's also used in **Happy Birthday - Selamat hari lahir** (Which, by the way, literally means Happy day born).*

Safe/Goodwill – Selamat
Imagine you want to buy a non-slip <u>safe</u> mat so you go to a bazar to find a <u>seller</u> of <u>mats</u>.

Malaysians break the day up like we do into four divisions, Morning, Afternoon, Evening and Night but the word for Evening and Night is the same.

The word **Selamat** is used in front of the following words to make Good morning, Good Afternoon, Good Evening or Night.

Morning – Pagi
Imagine you get up in the <u>morning</u>, look in the mirror and your eyes are all <u>baggy</u>.

Afternoon – Tengah hari
Imagine you say <u>good afternoon</u> to your neighbour who is making a barbeque with a <u>tong</u> which is all <u>hairy</u>.

Evening – Petang (Pr: Pe tang)
Imagine you relax in the <u>Evening</u> stroking your cat who <u>purr</u>s and sticks her <u>tongue</u> out.

Night – Malam (When it's dark)
Imagine you go out clubbing every <u>night</u> with your sheep who's a great break dancer, you tell everyone who's watching, that's <u>ma' lamb.</u>

Practice these every day and you'll soon find they become second nature.

To say goodbye we also use Selamat but with Tinggal or Jalan depending whether you are leaving or someone else is leaving.

If you are leaving!

Goodbye – Selamat tinggal (Lit: "Safe continued existence")
Imagine saying <u>goodbye</u> as you leave the shop of a wonderful <u>seller</u> of <u>mat</u>s who makes you <u>tingle</u>.

If someone else is leaving!

Goodbye – Selamat Jalan (Lit: "Safe travels")
Imagine saying <u>goodbye</u> to the <u>Jay</u> bird called <u>Alan</u> as he flies away.

Checking what you've learned

English	Malaysian
Evening	Petang
Good luck	Selamat
Night	Malam
Goodbye (You leave)	Selamat tinggal
Morning	Pagi
Afternoon	Tengah hari
Safe/Goodwill	Selamat
Goodbye (Others leave)	Selamat Jalan

Helpful Tips

You can also say Pagi-Pagi for early morning. The time when you will get the best price (morning price) at the market, (Harga pagi).

Phrases & Slang out and about

How's it going?

There are quite a few phrases Malaysians use that don't make much sense when literally translated, but are used in everyday conversation and greetings. The most common you will hear is:

"Mahu ke mana" – literally Want to where!

It's really asking – **"where are you going"** – which, to some Western cultures can appear a bit invasive and elicit a response like – "What business is it of yours?" However, it's more akin to **"How's it going"**, the usual response is, **"Jalan-jalan"** which means **"around"**. This saves you feeling like you have to tell the person details about your life, and will, surprisingly, be quite acceptable to them.

Jalan, as you know, means **Road** (or **Route**), **Jalan-jalan** means **walk** or **going around**. It's like they are asking you **"how's it going"**, and you say, **"Oh I'm hanging out"**.

You'll also hear **"Dari Mana"** when you arrive from somewhere, like when you're coming home. This means, literally, **"From where"**. Again, it can appear invasive to sensitive types, but it's really just a greeting, they rarely actually want to know.

You can reply **"Baik"** – **"I'm OK"** or as before **"Jalan-jalan"** or **"Dari jalan-jalan"** – **"From around"**.

No Problem

You'll also hear this and probably use this often!

"Tidak apa" = **"Never mind"**

You've already met these words, but, because it's colloquial – it doesn't directly translate.

Literally this means **Not what.** *You might imagine some old British major in the 30's saying this and kind of making sense.*

There's a shortened version of this that you may hear:

"Tak-apa" = **"Never mind** or **Okay"**

The **Tidak** becomes **Tak** so it rolls off the tongue.

The next section gives you a few more of these colloquial and slang words that are often used in conversations and in text messaging.

Colloquial city and sms

There are many words in Malaysian that are readily spoken but you'll rarely find in language text books or even dictionaries. These have their influence mainly from Java and Bali and often originate from other languages such as Chinese, Portuguese and Dutch.

These words are spread by teen magazines and many radio and television programmes such as (in my opinion) the wonderfully badly acted Soaps (worth watching just for the over acting).

I'm only going to cover the most common here as there are many, however, this will help you understand when the speaker isn't taking into consideration that you are not a native.

The most frequent is the dropping of the initial letter or keeping the sound the same, for example:

Ini = ni

Itu = tu

Ya = ah

Also, in text messages, you may find these words used and-or the vowels dropped completely. This make it look like gobbledygook – however you can figure it out – see if you can work this out...

Nnti km prg k pntai?

Took me a while to unravel some of my friends' texts!

There are also quite a few words that are shortenings or modifications of existing words or expressions that stand in their own right.

Here are some slang words you may come across in general conversation and in text messages.

Slang	Description
Lah	This is used as an exclamation like saying – yeah in English. **I don't want that, yeah – Saya tak mahu tu, lah!**
Wah	Used as an exclamation when Lah just won't do. The exclamation is more of a - like in WOW!
Kan	We've covered this already in one use, as **isn't it** for emphasis of a statement but I've included it here for more detail. It can also be used to assert an agreement that you already have about something. **Itu kan rumah – yeah, that's the house.**
Tak	This is a shortening for **Tidak** – **Not**
Nak	This is commonly used to mean **one**, as in one of something.
Tak nak	Can you guess this from the above? Literally it's "Not one" which means – **I don't want it** (or this).

| **Ke** | Usually means "to" however it is often used to me "or", **This or that - Ni ke tu.** |

| **Belanja** | Generally meaning expense, this is also used to mean treat – as in at your expense! **Your treat? – Kamu belanja?** |

There are far too many to cover them all here so this is a taster of some phrases and slang you'll hear out and about to help you navigate the more common "street" view of the language.

Now let's practice using some of the new words we've learned...

Sentence practice part 1

Translate these sentences into Malaysian with the words you have learned so far. It's often much more simple than you expect. Malaysian is a common language for a country with a relatively low level of formal education and has a suitably uncomplicated structure.

Each practice section will help you to cement the words in your memory. Cheat as much as you like, it isn't a test, it's practice!

Translate this	Your Answer
Where is the doctors	
I want a bottle of water	
Yesterday I went for a swim	
I would like some ice cream	
I'd like a young coconut please	
Can I eat this	
What is this called	
I'm staying in the big house	
Who's that?	
When did you wake up	
Good evening, how's it going?	

You'll find typical answers are in the back of the book.

There's always more than one way to say the same thing and it's usually simpler than you think.

Some more great words to learn

Late for the dance party

Sun – Matahari
Imagine it doesn't <u>matter</u> if your friend <u>Harry</u> goes out in the <u>sun</u> as he's so hairy.

See/look - Melihat
Imagine you <u>look</u> to <u>see</u> the magician <u>Merlyn</u> in an outrageous <u>hat</u>.

Meet - Bertemu
Imagine you <u>meet</u> your friend <u>Bert</u> and <u>he moos</u> at you. <u>Bert, he moos</u>!

Late - Lambat
Imagine you are <u>late</u> receiving the latest table tennis bat made from Sheep, the new <u>Lamb</u> <u>Bat</u>.

Dance – Tarian
Imagine you go to a club to <u>dance</u> and your friend Ann is lagging behind, you exclaim "Don't <u>tarry Ann!</u>"

Clever – Pandai
Imagine you are in the kitchen cooking a <u>clever</u> Chinese hari kari recipe requiring you to shout <u>pan die</u> at the frying pan.

Find/Look for – Cari
Imagine you are in Rome <u>looking for</u> and want to <u>find</u> a <u>chariot</u> made of solid gold.

Party – Pesta
Imagine you make a spaghetti dish for your <u>party</u> and suddenly remember you need <u>Pesto</u>.

All – Semua
Imagine you are on holiday up in the mountains where you can see it <u>all</u>, but, from higher up you can <u>see more</u>.

Driver – Pemandu
Imagine you hire a <u>driver</u> and he's so good you want him to always drive you, you ask, "Be my <u>perman</u>ent driver <u>do</u>"

Near – Dekat (Pr: Der Cat)
Imagine being <u>near</u> someone covered in cats and you're allergic so you have to <u>de-cat</u> them!

Just now – Sebentar tadi
Imagine that only <u>just now</u> you <u>see</u> the <u>burnt</u> the <u>tar</u> your <u>daddy</u>.

Head – Kepala
Imagine you walk into a <u>Cap</u> <u>Parlour</u> and your <u>head</u> is so happy to find such a splendid place!

Bus – Bas
Imagine you get on a <u>bus</u> which is full of <u>Bass</u> fish.

Right – Kanan (Pr: Ka Nan)
Imagine you are turning <u>right</u> in a castle blindfold and you walk into a <u>cannon</u>.

Not yet – Belum
Imagine you are disappointed that you have planted some prize roses and you have <u>not yet</u> seen a single <u>b-loom</u>.

Every – Setiap
Imagine that <u>every</u> time you sit down you adjust your sofa using your new mobile phone app – the <u>Settee app</u>.

Checking what you've learned

English	Malaysian
See	Melihat
Bus	Bas
Find (Look for)	Cari
Not yet	Belum
All	Semua
Dance	Tarian
Late	Lambat
Head	Kepala
Right	Kanan
Every	Setiap
Near	Dekat
Meet	Bertemu
Just now	Sebentar tadi
Sun	Matahari
Driver	Pemandu
Clever	Pandai
Party	Pesta

Remember you can go back over any that haven't quite landed in your noggin (brain)!

White sand, weather and sauce

Table – Meja
Imagine you sit down at a very low <u>table</u> and are worried that you <u>may jar</u> your knee.

Month – Bulan
Imagine your surprise when every <u>month</u> you get sent a <u>bull an'</u> a huge bill for it.

River – Sungai (Pr: Soong Eye)
Imagine you are at a <u>river</u> and you see <u>some guy</u> swimming in it.

Milk – Susu
Imagine when you spill <u>milk</u> on your friend Sue's new suit, they are annoyed, you say "so <u>Sue, sue</u> me".

Turn (Switch) on – Hidupkan (also means alive and life)
Imagine your computer ran for its <u>life</u> and <u>hid up</u> a tree with a <u>can</u> of beer rather than <u>turn</u> <u>on</u>.

White - Putih
Imagine you must drink a <u>white</u> mug of <u>poo tea</u>. (Yuk)

Sand - Pasir
Imagine being at the beach and asking your friend to <u>pass</u> <u>here</u> that bucket of <u>sand</u>.

People/Person – Orang
Imagine your surprise when you see a <u>person</u> then a group of <u>people</u> with <u>orange</u> skin wandering around your office.

Forest – Hutan
Imagine you are in a <u>forest</u> at night and you hear a <u>hoot and</u> a cry from the tree tops.

(Did you figure it out? Orang-utans are literally Forest People!)

Lingo Links™ Language Learning
www.lingolinks.biz

Weather – Cuaca
Imagine you are feeling under the <u>weather</u> so you <u>chew a char</u>coal brick.

Sometimes – Kadang-kadang
Imagine your car <u>sometimes</u> makes a funny noise when you drive. You explain to the mechanic your <u>car</u> goes <u>dang</u> twice.

Sauce – Sos
Imagine English <u>sauce</u> being poured over your Malaysian flag.

Write - Tulis
Imagine you <u>write</u> a loving letter <u>to Liz</u> – your best friend.

Work – Kerja
Imagine you <u>work</u> in a cottage cheese factory and need to keep the <u>curd</u> in a big <u>jar</u>.

Open – Buka
Imagine you <u>open</u> your web browser to <u>book a</u> new exotic holiday.

Shop – Kedai
Imagine you left some curd in a <u>shop</u> and go in and ask "Do you have that curd I left here?"

Cheap – Murah (Pr: Moo Rah)
Imagine you are so <u>cheap</u> you won't pay for <u>more wrapping</u> for you presents.

Rent – Sewa
Imagine you hand over your <u>rent</u> from your special <u>saver</u> account.

Checking what you've learned

English	Malaysian
Shop	Kedai
Sauce	Sos
Milk	Susu
Open	Buka
Work	Kerja
Month	Bulan
White	Putih
Write	Tulis
River	Sungai
Sand	Pasir
Turn (Switch) on	Hidupkan
Cheap	Murah
Sometimes	Kadang-kadang
Rent	Sewa
People	Orang
Table	Meja
Forest	Hutan
Weather	Cuaca

Yes – you did it – you remembered more Malaysian words.

Remember to congratulate yourself for what you remembered!

More words for your Malaysian journey

Sorry for the rain and mosquitoes

Sorry – Ma-af (Pr: *With a glottal stop as in Uh-oh*)
Imagine you are going to hospital and feel <u>sorry</u> to see your <u>Ma</u> <u>af</u>ter her painful operation.

Mosquito – Nyamuk (Pr: Ne Ya Mook)
Imagine you are exploring a bog and get stung by a <u>mosquito</u> in <u>the muck</u>.

Rain – Hujan
Imagine the <u>rain</u> caused a tidal wave of water while you are on holiday, it's <u>huge and</u> full of rubbish.

ATM – ATM
Imagine you go to the <u>Cash machine</u> in Malaysia and it says <u>ATM</u> on the machine – joy!

Peanut – Kacang
Imagine you are at circus and a monkey is throwing <u>peanuts</u> at you which you must <u>catch</u> and <u>hang</u> them on a washing line.

Fan – Kipas (Pr: Key Pas)
Imagine you are really hot and have a <u>fan</u> blowing smelly air on you because the blades are made of <u>Kippers</u>.

Fast – Cepat (cepat)
Imagine how <u>fast</u> you can run to the chip shop when you are wearing your new streamlined <u>chip hat</u>.

Flower(s) – Bunga (bunga)
Imagine your disgust when you give your Mum some <u>flowers</u> and she <u>bung the</u> lot in the dustbin.

Everywhere – Di mana-mana (Pr: Dee Man Ah-Man Ah)
Imagine a Manor shaped like a D is here and here and here,
<u>everywhere</u> you go there's a <u>D-manor</u> and another <u>D-manor</u>.

Favourite – Kegemaran (Pr: Ker Ger Ma Ran)
Imagine your <u>favourite</u> ice cream <u>curdle</u>d when you
<u>Ma ran</u> down the street with it.

Often - Sering
Imagine your Dad got knighted and often telephones to brag
about it. <u>Sir rings</u> you too <u>often</u>.

Like – Suka (Pr: Sue Ka)
Imagine you really <u>like</u> your crazy cousin even though he's a
<u>sucker</u>.

After – Selepas
Imagine you are at the market and <u>after</u> letting the <u>seller pass</u>,
you can get through to the stalls.

How long (time) - Berapa lama
Imagine someone asking <u>how long</u> the <u>Bear Rapper</u>s met the Dali
<u>Lama</u> for.

Orange (Fruit) – Oren *(Fruit)*
Imagine you are on a hike and use an <u>Orange</u> as a compass to
<u>orien</u>tate yourself.

Delicious – Sedap
Imagine you are in a restaurant having such a <u>delicious</u> meal you
can't <u>sit up</u> anymore so you slide under the table in ecstasy.

Sick/Pain - Sakit
Imagine you are in hospital <u>sick</u> and in <u>pain</u> after you fell on the
<u>Sack Kit</u> you bought to make sacks with.

Try – Cuba (Pr: Chew ba)
Imagine you <u>try</u> to some old chocolate but it's so tough you can't
<u>chew</u> the <u>bar</u>.

Checking what you've learned

English	Malaysian	
Often	Sering	
Try	Cuba	
Like	Suka	
Fan	Kipas	
Everywhere	Di mana-mana	
Orange (Fruit)	Oren	
Sorry	Ma-af	
Sick/Pain	Sakit	
How long (time)	Berapa lama	
Delicious	Sedap	
Rain	Hujan	
Mosquito	Nyamuk	
Fast	Cepat (cepat)	
Peanut	Kacang	
After	Selepas	
Flower(s)	Bunga (bunga)	
ATM	ATM	
Favourite	Kegemaran	

Remember you can go back over any that haven't quite landed!

Yes you can learn many words

Rubbish Taxi's and a place to sleep

Sleep – Tidur (Pr: Tid Oor)
Imagine you have to <u>sleep</u> on <u>the</u>
<u>door</u> for your bad back.

Rubbish – Sampah
Imagine your friend Sam dresses up
in old rags and you ask your Dad, is that <u>rubbish</u> or is it <u>Sam Pa</u>?

Orange (Colour) – Jingga
Imagine just bought an <u>Orange</u> coloured <u>Gin</u> in a <u>ga</u>rage sale.

Place – Tempat (Pr: Temp At)
Imagine you have a <u>place</u> reserved for your bike and it's broken
because someone has <u>tampered</u> with it.

Bed – Katil
Imagine your <u>cat</u> is <u>ill</u> so you let her sleep on the <u>bed</u>. Ahhh!

Credit for phone – Top up
Imagine you are delighted how cheap the <u>Top up</u> for your phone
is.

Taxi – Teksi
Imagine you call a <u>Taxi</u> and it turns up painted with
a Malaysian flag.

Money – Wang/Duit
Imagine all your <u>money</u> is counterfeit and you had to <u>do it</u> in
your garage so yo<u>u hang</u> it out of the window to dry.

Ago - Masa lalu
Imagine telling your friend that a long time <u>ago</u> you could get a
<u>massage</u> in <u>La Lou</u>vre.

Originate - Berasal
Imagine your shock while doing family research that you discover you <u>origi</u>nate from a rare breed of <u>bur</u>nt Jack <u>Russell</u>.

Dry – Kering
Imagine you go out for a walk and get soaked through and the only thing that stays <u>dry</u> is your <u>key ring</u>.

Shoes – Kasut
Imagine you bought some special <u>shoes</u> to go with your new <u>cat</u> <u>suit</u>.

Yellow – Kuning (Pr: Koo Ning)
Imagine you paint yourself <u>yellow</u> as a <u>cunning</u> way to attract a mate.

Usual/Ordinary – Biasa
Imagine your friends think your behaviour is quite <u>ordinary</u> when as <u>usual</u> you go to a fancy dress to <u>be as a</u> fairy.

Need – Perlu
Imagine you live in a Palace and so <u>need</u> to buy a toilet made of pearl, a <u>pearl loo</u>.

Must – Mesti
Imagine you <u>must</u> clean out your wardrobe because it's got really <u>musty</u>.

Make/Build – Buat
Imagine you are destitute so <u>make</u> a cake and <u>build</u> a house out of it which is so horrible, people <u>boo at</u> it.

Only – Hanya/Cuma
Imagine you are a dog and <u>only</u> like to <u>hang ya</u> head out of the car window when you can <u>chew ma</u> bone.

Checking what you've learned

English	Malaysian
Ago	Masa lalu
Bed	Katil
Rubbish	Sampah
Originate	Berasal
Only	Hanya/Cuma
Sleep	Tidur
Orange (Colour)	Jingga
Taxi	Taxi
Make/Build	Buat
Must	Mesti
Yellow	Kuning
Usual	Biasa
Credit for phone	Top up
Place	Tempat
Dry	Kering
Shoes	Kasut
Money	Wang/Duit
Need	Perlu

Congratulate yourself for what you remembered and you'll train your brain to be happy to remember more.

Get ready to start the download

Start – Bermula
Imagine you are so happy to start your journey to Bermuda you sing a little Laa.

Besides – Selain
Imagine you go to your local Zoo and they have a special on so that you can sit beside the Sea Lion.

Fire – Api
Imagine you are a pyromaniac and spend ages trying to set fire to a pea.

Plan – Rancangan
Imagine you have a plan and you rang Channon's gang to check it was OK.

Help (assist) – Bantuan
Imagine you are oversubscribed by Ann's and need help to ban two Ann's from your chess club.

Emotion – Emosi
Imagine your deeply felt emotion about your dead gold fish was cut short to just an emoti.

Go out/Exit – Keluar
Imagine you go out to your language class and the teacher tells you to curl your R.

Ready (get ready) - Bersedia
Imagine you are getting ready to pay your College fees and ask, "Where's the Bursar dear?"

Safe – Selamat
Imagine you want to buy a non-slip safe mat so you go to a bazar to find a seller of mats.

Olive – Zaitun
Imagine you hear a Greek man <u>sigh</u> as the <u>ton</u> of <u>Olives</u> you are loading onto his boat drops into the sea.

Listen – Dengar
Imagine you <u>listen</u> to the horrible noise your neighbour makes building a <u>den</u> in his <u>gar</u>den with a chain saw.

Download – Muat turun
Imagine you buy a new voice activated computer and you must <u>Moo at</u> it <u>to run</u> a download.

Religion – Agama
Imagine you are a despot and start a new <u>religion</u> to aggravate mothers called <u>Aga Ma.</u>

Jar – Jar
Imagine you feel exuberant and so buy a designer <u>jar</u> which looks like a map of Indonesia.

Something – Sesuatu
Imagine you need <u>something</u> from town and your friend says she'll get it if she <u>sees</u> <u>you at two.</u>

Rarely – Jarang
Imagine you <u>rarely</u> call your African friend and when you do he's so happy he says, "Great man, <u>ja rang</u>!"

About – Mengenai
Imagine you are <u>about</u> to come home with your friend (who is a Mung Bean). <u>Mung and I</u> are <u>about</u> to come home.

Different – Berbeza
Imagine you disguise yourself and look so <u>different</u> in your new <u>bird bed, a</u> bird comes and joins you.

Checking what you've learned

English	Malaysian	
Listen	Dengar	
Besides	Selain	
Fire	Api	
Different	Berbeza	
Something	Sesuatu	
Start	Bermula	
Emotion	Emosi	
Go out/Exit	Ke luar	
Ready (get ready)	Bersedia	
Help (assist)	Bantuan	
About	Mengenai	
Rarely	Jarang	
Religion	Agama	
Safe	Selamat	
Plan	Rancangan	
Olive	Zaitun	
Download	Muat turun	
Jar	Jar	

You can go back over any that haven't quite remembered!

Sentence practice part 2

Translate some more sentences into Malaysian with the words you have learned up to this point. Remember that Malaysian sentence structure is much simpler than English, and you'll probably need less words than you expect!

It's also a good time to go back over your answers to the last sentence practice, and translate them back into English.

Translate this	Your Answer
Stop here please	
I want to rent a room/house	
I don't feel well	
Where is a good place to eat?	
Sorry, I don't understand	
No peanuts please, I'm allergic	
Excuse me, I need a fork	
Where is the market?	
Where can I find an ATM?	
That was delicious	
Is it safe here at night	
How much to go to the Airport	

You'll find typical answers are in the back of the book.

Help-ful Tips

Practice different ways of saying the same thing - it's usually simpler than you think...

Unusual Foods and fruits

In Malaysia you will find many foods unusual to you. The most surprising for me were the fruits. I've included a few for you so you know what to expect and can ask for them by name. If you want the best deals, get down to the market at around five thirty in the morning.

Snake Fruit – Salak.

This fruit has a snake like pattern skin – hence the common name. It has a woody texture and a nutty flavour, a little like a chestnut. Makes a nice snack.

Pomelo – Jeruk Bali

Think of an enormous grapefruit that tastes of a mild orange. These fruit are very refreshing and have a thick skin and pith. Peeling one is an art requiring a sharp knife and patience.

Papaya – Papaya (Pepaya)

A Papaya is a large (often longer than your fore arm) orange coloured sweet fruit. It's a favourite for smoothies being easily peeled and liquidised. Contains seeds which are said to have digestive properties (at your own risk!)

Sour Sop - Sirsak

This fruit is a spiky (but not sharp) green fruit with a white stringy meat. Has been claimed to have health properties as a cure for cancer. Although this may be an exaggeration by the producers, it does appear to have some properties similar to chemo treatment without the side effects. (Your own research is recommend!)

Jack Fruit - Nangka

Jackfruit is a common fruit for Asia and Australia and considered as one of the largest tree borne fruit in the world. The juicy pulp around the seeds have a taste similar to pineapple, but milder. Apart from canned jackfruit, it is also available as sweet chips. The wood of the tree is used for making various musical instruments, while the fruit is a common ingredient for many Asian dishes.

Mangosteen - Manggis

The mangosteen is an evergreen tree that produces oddly shaped fruits. The fruits are purple outside, creamy inside, described as citrus with a hint of peach. It is rich in antioxidants, some scientists even suggesting it can lower risk against cancer. Don't eat too many at once though, as it can be used to aid constipation!

Rambutan - Rambutan

Coming from an evergreen tree, the Rambutan fruit resembles the Lychee, has a leathery red skin and is covered with spines. Rambutan is a popular garden fruit tree and one of the most famous in Southeast Asia. The fruit is sweet and juicy, being commonly found in jams or available canned. Rambutan literally means "hairy".

Durian - Durian

Also known as the "King of Fruits," Durian has a very particular odour (it stinks), a unique taste and is covered by a sharp spiky husk. Its smell is often compared to skunk spray or sewage so the fruit is often forbidden in hotels and on public transportation. Still, the whole experience is worth it considering the absolutely divine taste of the Durian. Tastes a bit like custard to me!

Noni – Noni

Another smelly fruit – this fruit is another claimed "Super Fruit" high in anti-oxidants. It is most often sold in powder form as a food supplement as the fruit itself does not taste good. The green fruit, leaves, and roots were traditionally used in Polynesian cultures to treat menstrual cramps, bowel irregularities, diabetes, liver diseases, and urinary tract infections. Try it for yourself!

Never, ever and possessions.

How to use ever and never.

The word for **Ever** in Malaysian is **Pernah**, however, there is no word for **Never**. Instead you simply negate **Ever** using **Tidak**. **Never**, is **Tidak pernah**!

Ever - Pernah
Imagine your friend asks you if you <u>ever</u> had a perm and you explain, a <u>perm na,</u> no way

For example:

> **You ever go to the beach? = Awak pernah pergi ke pantai?**

> **No, I never go.   = Tidak, saya tidak pernah pergi**

See what sentences you can make up using **Pernah** and **Tidak Pernah**.

How to indicate possessions and "the"

You've already come across the suffix **"nya"** in some of the words that you've learned but probably not realised that it is actually a modifier, not actually part of the root word.

The suffix, -**nya** is used to denote a relationship to the subject or object being mentioned. The relationship either describes possession (yours or mine) or refers to an object recently mentioned.

For example:

>   **What is that called?**   = **Apa nama*nya* itu?**

You can think of it as **"of"** or **"the"**... What is **the** name **of** that?

It's the same when asking the price of something.

>   **How much is it?**   =   **Berapa harga*nya*?**

And as **"the"** when referring to the subject of the conversation.

>   **Do you want to buy the car?** = **Kamu mahu beli kereta?**

And used for possession as **his, hers or theirs.**

>   **Jared went to his house.** = **Jared pergi ke rumah*nya*.**

>   **That's her book.**   = **Itu buku*nya*.**

*Have fun with it, it works for any object (noun). It requires good listening skills as it often makes the word sounds like a new word, when in fact it's one you already know with **nya** on the end.*

Lingo Links™ Language Learning
www.lingolinks.biz

You can remember so many more...

Sit down, have a Coffee

Come – Datang (Pr: Der Tung)
Imagine you <u>come</u> around to kissing with <u>the tongue</u> but not with your Granny.

Coffee – Kopi
Imagine you buy a <u>Coffee</u> and are so thirsty you <u>copy</u> it on the photocopier.

Until – Sehingga
Imagine at your birthday party can't wait <u>until</u> <u>the</u> <u>singer</u> arrives.

Spicy - Pedas
Imagine you go into a shop and ask for a <u>spicy</u> <u>pet arse</u>. *(Why wouldn't you!)*

This - Ini
Imagine you are in <u>this</u> new band and can't play a song because it's not <u>in E.</u>

Happy - Bahagia
Imagine you are very <u>happy</u> that your new top is <u>baggier</u> than your old one.

In/At/On - Di
Imagine you are <u>in</u> trouble <u>deep</u> when you forget to leave your tax return <u>on</u> the table <u>at</u> the Tax Office.

Left - Kiri
Imagine to turn <u>left</u> in the video game you are playing there is a <u>key</u> <u>r</u>equired.

Before - Sebelum
Imagine you are training to be a doctor but <u>before</u> you can be a brain surgeon you must remove the "R" from the cerebellum so it's a <u>ceebelum.</u>

Lingo Links™ Language Learning
www.lingolinks.biz

Take care – Jaga diri
Imagine you at a zoo and you tell your wife, take care, that's a <u>Jaguar</u> <u>dearie</u>.

Sure – Pasti
Imagine you are <u>sure</u> your stomach cramps are from a bad <u>pasty</u> you ate last night.

Fat – Gemuk (Pr: Geh Muk)
Imagine your disgust as your <u>fat</u> friend eats too much cake, explodes and it <u>get</u>s <u>muck</u> all over the living room.

Brother – Saudara laki-laki
Imagine you are happy when your little <u>Brother</u> goes to <u>Sud</u>i <u>Ara</u>bia on a business trip you sing he should be so lucky-lucky.

Day - Hari
Imagine one <u>day</u> you wake up discover, to your surprise, your name is actually <u>Harry</u>!

Broken – Rosak
Imagine your disappointment when you buy a <u>ruck</u>sack you buy for an expedition to the North Pole is <u>broken</u>.

Mother – Emak/Mak
Imagine your <u>Mother</u> coming into your room and saying, "Look at the <u>muck</u> in here".

On/Above – Atas
Imagine you are feeling precarious flying <u>on</u> a table high <u>above</u> the clouds being held up by an <u>At</u>las.

Upstairs – Di atas (Lit: in above)
Imagine you are <u>upstairs</u> and someone has fumigated upstairs with anti-Atlas smoke, the place is being <u>de-At</u>lased.

Lingo Links™ Language Learning
www.lingolinks.biz

Checking what you've learned

English	Malaysian
Until	Sehingga
On/Above	Atas
This	Ini
Happy	Bahagia
Take care	Jaga diri
Mother	Emak/Mak
Spicy	Pedas
Brother	Saudara laki-laki
Upstairs	Di atas
Before	Sebelum
Broken	Rosak
Sure	Pasti
Coffee	Kopi
Come	Datang
Day	Hari
In/At/On	Di
Left	Kiri
Fat	Gemuk

Remember to go back over any that haven't quite landed!

Old pancakes and black phones

Wet – Basah
Imagine going to your school Bazaar and it rains so hard you get very wet.

Old (Age) – Tua
Imagine you are doing some charity work taking to group of old people to a ball.

Difficult – Sukar
Imagine how difficult it was to clean the split sugar out of your laptop.

Quiet (Calm) – Tenang
Imagine how quiet it was at your party when you managed to get ten noisy kids hung out of the window. *(I know you wouldn't!)*

Pancake – Penkek
Imagine you make a pancake out of pens, it's pen cake!

Best – Terbaik
Imagine you go to a bike show and see the best turbo bike you ever saw!

Dentist – Doktor gigi
Imagine going to the alternative Dentist to have your teeth out and the vibrating doctor gives you the giggles.

Cake – Kek
Imagine you really want to buy cake that looks like a Malaysian flag.

Mobile Phone – Telefon bimbit
Imagine leant your Mobile phone to a telethon bimbo and she bit through it 'cause she thought it was a bar of chocolate.

Expensive – Mahal
Imagine you go for a cruise in your expensive boat to visit the Taj Mahal.

Lingo Links™ Language Learning
www.lingolinks.biz

Far – Jauh
Imagine you want to go out to see an old age battle but it's really <u>far</u> to the local castle to see the Knights <u>Joust</u>.

Bank – Bank
Imagine your French friend works in a <u>bank</u>, he calls it a <u>Banque</u>!

Electricity – Listrik
Imagine your friend Liz does a magic trick with <u>electricity</u>, which she describes as a <u>Liz trick</u>.

Friend - Rakan
Imagine your cool <u>friend</u> has a really great <u>rack and</u> knows how to fix it to the car. *(What were **you** thinking?* ☺ *)*

Sweet - Manis
Imagine you are at the circus watch the strong act and you cannot believe how many <u>sweets</u> that <u>man is</u> carrying.

Woman – Wanita
Imagine you are going to see a <u>woman</u> who is the world record holder for eating. That's <u>one</u> big <u>eater</u>.

Sister – Saudara perempuan
Imagine your joy as your <u>Sister</u> has won a trip to the <u>Saharah</u>. *(Followed by the word for Woman above)*

Checking what you've learned

English	Malaysian
Old (Age)	Tua
Pancake	Penkek
Sister	Saudara perempuan
Wet	Basah
Best	Terbaik
Difficult	Sukar
Dentist	Dokter gigi
Cake	Kek
Friend	Rakan
Quiet (Calm)	Tenang
Mobile Phone	Telefon bimbit
Expensive	Mahal
Sweet	Manis
Woman	Wanita
Bank	Bank
Electricity	Listrik
Far	Jauh

Nice one – you've got even more Malaysian words installed.

Please congratulate yourself on what you remembered!

How to say I'm doing that first

When someone asks you if you want to do something, and you say, "I want to do this first", in Malaysian we use the term **dulu**.

In this case it is being used like the word **before** or **ago**.

Generally, just think of it as **first** (as in doing that first) and you'll get your meaning across (and understand theirs).

First/Before - Dahulu
Imagine <u>first</u>, <u>before</u> you go out your child needs the toilet but can't because it's <u>Dad</u> <u>who</u> is in the <u>loo</u>.

For example:

I want to sleep first.	=	Saya mahu tidur dadulu.
I want to eat first.	=	Saya mahu makan dadulu.
Have you been here before?	=	Kamu pernah di sini dahulu?

There are many ways to say the same thing, that's the beauty of language. But remember, to understand what is being said, it's useful to know the various ways words can be used.

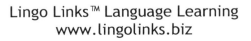

Chat ups, romance and lovers!

Darling, I love your eyes

This section will help you connect more easily with that love you always wanted! Why is this section so late in the book? How could I be so mean? Well, it's to keep you motivated. Of course, some of you, (like I did with my first phrase book) will jump straight to this section. It's a great start – but remember, you might want something more to talk about later! Good luck.

Love – Cinta *(Remember c is pronounced ch)*
Imagine you love having a <u>chin</u> covered in <u>tar</u>.

Darling – Sayang *(like honey or sweetheart Pr: Sigh Ang)*
Imagine being delighted with your <u>darling</u> <u>sweetheart</u> who agrees with everything you are <u>saying</u>.

Beautiful – Cantik
Imagine how <u>beautiful</u> it is when your football team <u>chants</u> "<u>Ik</u>" for their new player Ickey.

Eyes – Mata
Imagine being happy when your doctor tells you there is nothing the <u>matter</u> with your <u>eyes</u>.

Cool – Sempoi *(Impressive)*
Imagine being <u>cool</u> that you saw the <u>same boy </u>as last week.

Sexy – Seksi
Imagine you look so sexy wrapped in a Malaysian flag.

Hug – Pelukan (Pr: Pr Loo Can)
Imagine you are feeling amorous and so you go to the zoo and <u>hug</u> a giant <u>Pelikan</u>.

Girlfriend – Teman wanita
Imagine your <u>girlfriend</u> is <u>the man</u> and a <u>man eater</u>!

Film – Filem
Imagine you go to a film and you see nothing but a Malaysian flag on the screen for an hour!

Dinner – Makan malam
Imagine for <u>dinner</u> you <u>make an</u> excuse for burping while eating my <u>lamb!</u>

Walk – Jalan-jalan
Imagine you have a long <u>walk</u> ahead of you and it's a <u>challenge</u>, a real <u>challenge</u>.

Holiday – Cuti
Imagine you go on <u>holiday</u> to Turkey where you have to <u>chew</u> the <u>tea</u> it's so strong.

Husband – Suami
Imagine your <u>husband</u> is from India and is a <u>Swami</u>.

Bad – Buruk
Imagine you believe it's <u>bad</u> to cross a <u>brook</u> in a forest without paying the brook goblin.

Married – Berkahwin
Imagine are married to a <u>berk</u> wh<u>o</u> <u>win</u>s at everything.

Wife – Isteri
Imagine you broke up with your <u>Wife</u>, and tell your friends that your wife is <u>history</u>.

Boyfriend – Teman lelaki
Imagine you boyfriend is <u>the man</u> and <u>let</u>s you be <u>lucky</u>.

Watch – Tengok
Imagine you want so much to <u>watch</u> your favourite show at <u>ten</u> o'<u>clock</u>.

Checking what you've learned

English	Malaysian
Married	Berkahwin
Wife	Isteri
Darling	Sayang
Sexy	Seksi
Holiday	Cuti
Cool	Sempoi
Beautiful	Cantik
Bad	Buruk
Girlfriend	Teman wanita
Love	Cinta
Walk	Jalan-jalan
Hug	Pelukan
Boyfriend	Teman lelaki
Husband	Suami
Watch	Tengok
Film	Filem
Dinner	Malam makan
Eyes	Mata

Rock on – you did it!

Remember to can go back over any that haven't quite stuck if you're feeling up to it.

Sentence practice part 3

Practice your translations with the sentences below.

It's also a good time to go back over your answers to the last sentence practice, and translate them back into English.

Remember to congratulate yourself for what you remembered!

Translate this	Your Answer
Is this the road to Kuala Lumpur?	
This is my friend John	
I want a quiet room	
Look into my eyes	
Are you married?	
Is it far to the shops?	
Please massage my feet	
I have two older sisters	
That's cool	
I'm watching a film tonight	
Want to go dancing later?	

Suggested answers in the back as always.

Words on the home straight

Is it true your Father smells?

Father - Bapa
Imagine you are not worried that your
Father is lost in the shopping mall because
he's wearing his backpack.

Fix/Repair - Membaiki
Imagine you fix your speedo on your bike to
or as you like to say, mend biky!

New - Baru
Imagine you are feeling friendly so you let
your new neighbour use you wheel barrow.

Hand(s) - Tangan
Imagine your gang wondering why your hands are so brown and
you telling them it's because you left your hands out in the sun
to tan gang.

Towel - Tuala
Imagine you are about to pray and in your religion you have to
point your towel to Alah.

Older sibling - Kakak
Imagine at dinner your older brother or sister (sibling) regresses
to a child and screams for their cake-cake.

Close(d) - Tutup (Pr: Too Toop)
Imagine you work for the circus and need to tap a box full of
clown masks to close it.

Feet/Foot/Legs - Kaki
Imagine you are decorating naked, fell over a tin of paint and
now your legs and feet are khaki.

Stomach – Perut
Imagine after your favourite meal your stomach is happy so it purrs and hoots.

Jug – Jag
Imagine your buy a Jug in the shape of a wild Jaguar. Grrrr.

School – Sekolah (Pr: Sec Ol Ah)
Imagine going to school and studying so hard you become a scholar.

Police – Polis
Imagine you have a big mug of Police that you take a drink from and it tastes all policey.

Straight on – Lurus (Pr: Lur Oose)
Imagine thinking we want to go straight on but are afraid that a ghost wants to lure us round the corner.

Worry – Khuatir
Imagine outside a concert you worry about why it's so quiet here.

True/Indeed – Benar
Imagine it's true, that sticks when bent are better boomerangs than straight ones.

Smell – Bau
Imagine how crazy you feel because you have a new craving to smell the bow of a tree.

Again – Lagi
Imagine you have rats in the roof so are once again in the loft lagging the rafters after the rats have eaten it all.

Black – Hitam (Pr: Hit Um)
Imagine your excitement at your first baseball game when you see a guy in a black jersey hit and run home.

Checking what you've learned

English	Malaysian
Smell	Bau
Hands	Tangan
Jug	Jag
New	Baru
Older sibling	Kakak
Towel	Tuala
Again	Lagi
Police	Polis
Close(d)	Tutup
Fix	Membaiki
School	Sekolah
Feet/Foot/Legs	Kaki
Black	Hitam
True/Indeed	Benar
Stomach	Perut
Worry	Khuatir
Father	Bapa
Straight on	Lurus

Remember you can go back over any that you haven't quite learned!

Small change for your family under the tree

So - Jadi
Imagine you know it is <u>so</u> like that Boss to <u>jar the</u> door open on a cold day!

Tree - Pokok (Pr: Poh cock)
Imagine you are on a walk in the woods and are surprised to see a <u>Pea</u><u>cock</u> in a <u>tree</u>.

Younger sibling - Adik
Imagine your <u>younger Brother or Sister</u> is showing off to your friends and being a bit of <u>a dick</u>.

Man - Lelaki
Imagine you know a French <u>man</u> who is so fortunate they call him <u>Le Lucky</u> (The lucky).

Small - Kecil (Pr: Ker Chill)
Imagine you go to a miniature museum see a really <u>small</u> doll of <u>Churchill</u>.

Loose change - Wang kecil
Imagine yo<u>u hang Churchill</u> out the window to shake some <u>loose change</u> from his pockets.

Inside - Dalam (within)
Imagine you are <u>inside</u> a lamp with a genie <u>within</u> <u>the lamp</u> of Ali-Baba.

Letter - Surat (Pr: Sue Rat)
Imagine you receive a <u>letter</u> from your favourite animal Knight - <u>Sir Rat</u>.

Newspaper - Surat khabar (Lit: Letter News)
Imagine you read a heading in the <u>Newspaper</u> about the local tree throwing contest, <u>Sir Rat</u> throws <u>caber</u>.

Lingo Links™ Language Learning
www.lingolinks.biz

Children – kanak-kanak
Imagine all your <u>children</u> <u>ca</u>n have a <u>knack</u> of getting themselves into trouble at school.

Change – Ubah
Imagine you saw a huge <u>change</u> in your kids behaviour when y<u>ou</u> <u>bar</u>red them from eating chocolate.

Family – Keluarga
Imagine your <u>family</u> keeping warm around the new <u>colour Aga</u> cooker.

Under – Bawah
Imagine you duck <u>under</u> the <u>bow</u> of <u>a</u> tree on a walk through the woods.

Rice Field – Sawah
Imagine you are eating rice from the <u>rice field</u> before it is ripe and it tastes <u>sour</u>.

Tall – Tinggi
Imagine you are in India and you go to the famous <u>tall</u> landmark of a <u>tin</u> of <u>Ghee</u>. *(Ghee is Indian clarified butter, 'case ya didn't know)*

Turn – Belok
Imagine you are driving to work and need to <u>turn</u> as the road ahead has a <u>b-lock</u>.

Do – Lakukan
Imagine you need to <u>do</u> a paint job but you can't because you <u>lack a can</u>.

Allergy/Allergic – Alahan
Imagine your mate <u>Al</u> gives you <u>a</u> h<u>and</u> with your <u>allergy</u> problems by cutting the grass for you.

Checking what you've learned

English	Malaysian
Rice Field	Sawah
Tree	Pokok
Inside	Dalam
Man	Lelaki
So	Jadi
Do	Lakukan
Younger sibling	Adik
Loose change	Wang kecil
Tall	Tingi
Allergy	Alahan
Letter	Surat
Under	Bawah
Change	Ubah
Small	Kecil
Newspaper	Surat khabar
Children	Kanak-kanak
Family	Keluarga
Turn	Belok

You can congratulate yourself on what you remembered, go on, you deserve it.

Lingo Links™ Language Learning
www.lingolinks.biz

Numbers & Money

Learning your numbers and all about money.

Malaysian numbers are just something you need to learn to get by. Because there are so many, it's best to learn them by counting and random practice. Once you have the measure of counting, you can try translating numbers randomly until you find you can recall any number at will.

The exchange rate is not so high, about 3.7 to the US Dollar, 5.5 to Sterling and 1.38 to the Euro. This means only a grasp of numbers into the thousands is necessary to handle money most money situations – but you never know your luck!

Start by learning the **units 1 to 10** then **11 to 19** and then the **tens, hundreds** and **millions**. They follow predictable patterns, so once you have the hang of that, it's quite straight forward!

One to Ten (1- 10)

One – Satu (Pr: Sar Too)
Imagine you are in Italy and you see <u>one</u> <u>statue</u> in the square.

Two – Dua
Imagine you like being but your <u>two</u> friends are real <u>doer</u>s.

Three – Tiga (Pr: Tee Gah)
Imagine you go to the zoo and see <u>three</u> ferocious <u>tiger</u>s in a cage.

Four - Empat
Imagine you are invited on a TV show because you have <u>four</u> sisters who are all <u>empat</u>hs.

Five - Lima
Imagine your surprise when you go home and there are <u>five</u> <u>Lima</u>s in your living room.

Six - Enam
Imagine you go to the jewellers to have <u>six</u> ornaments <u>enam</u>elled ready for display.

Seven – Tujuh
Imagine <u>seven</u> of your Jewish friends are not <u>too</u> <u>Jew</u>ish.

Eight – Lapan (Pr: La Pan)
Imagine you want to cook sitting down so you bought <u>eight</u> special <u>lap</u> <u>pan</u>s for your kitchen.

Nine - Sembilan
Imagine you go to a look-alike show and see <u>nine</u> people have a <u>semblan</u>ce to the Queen of England.

Ten - Sepuluh
Imagine you go to a club and one of <u>ten</u> knights try's to pick you up, <u>Sir</u> <u>pulls</u> <u>you</u>.

Checking your numbers

Numeral	English	Malaysian
1	One	Satu
2	Two	Dua
3	Three	Tiga
4	Four	Empat
5	Five	Lima
6	Six	Enam
7	Seven	Tujuh
8	Eight	Lapan
9	Nine	Sembilan
10	Ten	Sepuluh

Once you have learned to say the numbers in sequence from 1 to 10, take a pen and write numbers in a random order and translate them. This way you are able to recall numbers out of order like you will need to in real life.

Also, write the numbers in Malaysian in a random order and come back to the list in an hour or so and translate them back. This will help you translate randomly in both directions. *There's a practice section coming up if you are feeling lazy!*

Eleven to Nineteen (11 – 19)

In the table below you can see the pattern of using **belas** at the end of a base number to get the numbers **12 to 19**.

So, in this case, all you need to learn is **"Sebelas"** for eleven and you have the rest just from having learned **1 to 9**. Sweet!

Eleven – Sebelas
Imagine <u>eleven</u> knights ringing bells – they are <u>Sir Bellers</u>.

Numeral	English	Malaysian
11	Eleven	Sebelas
12	Twelve	Dua belas
13	Thirteen	Tiga belas
14	Fourteen	Empat belas
15	Fifteen	Lima belas
16	Sixteen	Enam belas
17	Seventeen	Tujuh belas
18	Eighteen	Lapan belas
19	Nineteen	Sembilan belas

Practicing with these numbers as before will help lodge the numbers **1 to 9** in your memory.

The tens (20, 30, 40....)

The tens from Twenty to Ninety follow a similar pattern. They are simply the units (2, 3, 4 etc.) followed by the word for **Ten** - **"Puluh"**.

Numeral	English	Malaysian
20	Twenty	Dua puluh
30	Thirty	Tiga puluh
40	Forty	Empat puluh
50	Fifty	Lima puluh
60	Sixty	Enam puluh
70	Seventy	Tujuh puluh
80	Eighty	Lapan puluh
90	Ninety	Sembilan puluh

You have all the numbers from **One** to **A Hundred** by learning just eleven more words. Yippee!

For the numbers between the Tens, simply say the unit you need. For example.

23 **Twenty - three** is **Dua puluh - tiga**

48 **Forty - Eight**   is **Empat puluh – lapan**

72 **Seventy – two**   is **Tujuh Puluh – Dua**

And so on...

Lingo Links™ Language Learning
www.lingolinks.biz

Hundreds, Thousands and Millions

Now all we need is three more words to count to Millions.

Hundred – Ratus
Imagine you live in a Rat kingdom and there are one hundred
<u>Rat</u>'s like <u>us.</u>

Thousand – Ribu
Imagine a <u>Thousand</u> people decide to <u>rib you</u> about your shoes.

Million – Juta
Imagine a Jew giving you a <u>million</u> dollars, and you thank them
appropriately saying, "<u>Jew ta</u>".

Here are some examples of writing larger numbers.

Numeral	English	Malaysian
100	One Hundred	Satu ratus
2,000	Two Thousand	Dua ribu
40,000	Forty Thousand	Empat puluh ribu
100,000	One Hundred Thousand	Satu ratus ribu
5,000,000	Five Million	Lima juta
300,000,000	Three Hundred Million	Tiga ratus juta

Use the table below as before to check what you've learned.

Numeral	English	Malaysian
100	Hundred	Ratus
1,000	Thousand	Ribu
1,000,000	Million	Juta

Now you can work out the rest!

Great - **WELL DONE** - you can now count to a million million - *(if you've got the time)*.

Ordinals and No. of times.

Ordinals are the words for **First**, **Second**, **Third** etc.

These are also very simple in Malaysian. Once you know your numbers, you only have to learn one more word to have all the ordinals. That word is the word for **First**.

First – Pertama
Imagine you win <u>first</u> prize in competition to make mothers more attractive and the competition is called <u>Pert a ma</u>!

All the other Ordinals are the number preceded by **Ke**. _Thanks again Malaysia for making the language so straight forward._

To say **Second** is **Ke**dua; **Third** is **Ke**tiga and so on...

You might also want to say the number of times something has happened, e.g. it happened once, twice, three times and so on. For this we need the word **Kali** which is used like the word "Times" in English but literally means **Time**.

Time – Kali
Imagine you have lost track of the number of <u>time</u>s you've told your mechanic that your <u>Car lea</u>ns to the left.

Now for Once, twice, three times etc. we add Kali

> **Once - Sekali** _(or Satu Kali – Lit: One time)_
> _(Did you remember that_ **Se-** _means_ **One?**_)_

> **Twice - Dua kali...**

Can you figure out how to say, "The third time"?   (Tip: use –nya)

Now let's check to see how much you've remembered...

Checking all your numbers....

Here's some numbers to translate – see how you get on...

Number	Translate this	Your Answer
24	Twenty four	
19	Nineteen	
5	Five	
n/a	Twice	
132	One hundred and thirty two	
2,000,000	Two Million	
1st	First	
7,000	Seven Thousand	
926	Nine hundred and twenty six	
81	Eighty one	
21st	Twenty first	

Write your answers down and cover the English over to practice translating them back.

Here's how to say **"The third time"** – **"Ketiga kalinya"**. We simply add the suffix -nya onto kali. Well done if you got it.

That's all the numbers and ordinals covered – Hope you got on well. Remember to congratulate yourself for what you remembered to keep up the positive reinforcement.

Now let's look at the Date and Time...

Date and Time

Months and Days of the week

We are lucky – the month names are very similar to months we already know in English. The spelling and pronunciation are slightly different but it's so close you could more or less get away with using the English words. The days of the week are quite different so for simplicity, we'll start with the Month names.

Month names

Month names are very similar to English month names as they are based on the same Roman Julian calendar that we use today. August is the only word that's slightly different – *you just drop the "t" at the end*.

The spelling is different in many cases, so, let's look at the months altogether...

Lingo Links™ Language Learning
www.lingolinks.biz

Month	Bulan
January	Januari
February	Februari
March	Mac
April	April
May	Mei
June	Jun
July	Julai
August	Ogos
September	September
October	Oktober
November	November
December	Disember

*The word for **Month** is **Bulan** (which also means moon) the cycle of which was the original derivation of a month. (The cycle of the moon averages 29.5 days by the way).*

What's the date?

The word for date is **Tanggal** – Imagine you are in a <u>tangle</u> from streamers on the <u>date</u> of your 30th year at work!

To say the date, it's the same as in British English but without the ordinal. E.g.

- 4th July – Empat Julai
- 1st March – Satu Mac
- 5th November – Lima November

It's much simpler than in English because you don't have to use the ordinals like 1st 2nd and 3rd in Malaysian.

Days of the week

Now let's learn the days of the week. Really get into the feeling, sense and imagery of doing of these things each week day.

Monday - Isnin
Imagine <u>Mondays</u> are days for <u>listening</u>.

Tuesday - Selasa
Imagine every <u>Tuesday</u> you go for <u>Salsa</u> lessons.

Wednesday - Rabu
Imagine <u>Wednesday</u> is the day to meet the <u>Rabi.</u>

Thursday - Khamis
Imagine <u>Thursday</u> is the day for wearing your <u>cami</u>sole. (It's a kind of underwear in case you didn't know)

Friday - Jumaat
Imagine <u>Fridays</u> you go <u>jam at</u> the local bar

Saturday - Sabtu
Imagine Saturday is the <u>Sabb</u>ath <u>too</u>

Sunday – Ahad (Minggu also means week)
Imagine on <u>Sunday</u> you need <u>a hat</u> to go to church.

Checking your days of the week

English	Malaysian
Wednesday	Rabu
Sunday	Ahad
Thursday	Khamis
Monday	Isnin
Saturday	Sabtu
Tuesday	Selasa
Friday	Jumaat

Remember you can go back over any that haven't quite landed!

Seasons

The climate in Malaysia is almost entirely tropical with a temperature remaining fairly stable around 22-32 degrees Celcius, dropping slightly in the dry season (especially at night). As a result, there are only really two distinct seasons, the Hot season which tends to be wet and the Cold season which is dry, the timing of which varies slightly by region.

Southwest (Inc Kuala Lumpur and Malacca)

- **Hot** season, from **October to April**
- **Cold** season from **May to September**.

Northeast

- **Hot** season, from **November to March**.
- **Cold** season from **April to October**

Season - Musim
Imagine you love history and so have bought a <u>season</u> ticket to the local <u>museum</u>.

Cold – Sejuk (Pr: Se jook)
Imagine you buy a <u>cold</u> drink and it'<u>s a joke</u> because it's still room temperature.

Hot – Panas
Imagine you need a <u>pan as</u> big as the sun the food is so <u>hot</u>

To say the season, you put the descriptive word after the word for season.

Hot Season is **Musim Panas**

Cold Season is **Musim Dingin**.

Ah – life is so simple in Malaysia!

Lingo Links™ Language Learning
www.lingolinks.biz

Telling the time

You're going to need your numbers for this, (at least up to 59), if you want to tell the time accurately. Mostly, I find I arrange things on the hour or half hour to make things easier.

To say the time you put the word for **o'clock (pukul)** after the time.

Pukul means to strike (as in hit) so it's like striking the hour!

O'clock/Strike – Pukul
Imagine every day you dog poos outside and when your clock <u>strikes</u> 10 <u>o'clock</u> the <u>poo</u> is <u>cool</u> enough to pick up and throw away. *(You'll never forget that one eh! ☺)*

For example:

- **1 o'clock** is **Pukul satu**
- **5 o'clock** is **Pukul lima**

Pretty easy – yeah!

Oh, and if you want to be clear on AM or PM just add morning or Afternoon on the end.

- **6 AM** is **Pukul enam pagi**
- **9 PM** is **Pukul sembilan malam**

So far so good, also, when you want to say the half hour the Malaysians use the same approach to English. They say half and then the hour. So, 3:30 would be half three.

Half is **Setengah** so to say **4:30** is **empat setengah**

You can of course quote the time in digital watch format so 7:50 would be... well, by now I'm sure you can work it out!

It's **Jam tujuh lima puluh** – **Seven fifty** - just in case you skipped the numbers section.

Time durations

When referring to duration of time we'll need to know the words for hour, minute and second's as well.

Hour/Clock/Watch – Jam
Imagine every <u>hour</u> you get your <u>watch</u> covered in <u>Jam</u>.

Minute - Minit
Imagine you have to wait a <u>minute</u> under a
Malaysian flag.

Second - Saat
Imagine your joy when you <u>sat</u> <u>at</u> a bus stop for only a <u>second</u> before the bus came.

To say **two hours, seconds or minutes** is just like in English, **dua jam, minit, saat.**

If we want to say **two and a half hours, minutes or seconds**, it's a little different, for example.

Two and a half hours – dua jam setengah.

We need to put the "half" after the unit of time.

All this applies to Year, Month and Week also so you can now tell the time and how long you've been somewhere.

Sentence practise part 4

You can use many of the words you have learned to say so much.

Have a go at translating these sentences into Malaysian. Also, think about some of the things you might want to say, write them down and translate them. Keeping in mind, there are many ways to say the same thing.

It's also a good time to go back over your answers to the last sentence practice, and translate them back into English. Don't forget; you can always go back over any words that haven't quite landed to make sure they are in your memory.

Translate this	Your Answer
I just got back from the village	
Really, it was only twenty thousand Rupiah yesterday!	
I would love to meet your family	
I will meet you at 5:30pm	
I'm looking for a house for 4 million a month or less	
Yes, turn left by the big tree	
What are you doing right now?	
I want to move out on January 2nd	
This is my second stay in Bali	

You can check your answers in the back of the book.

Lingo Links™ Language Learning
www.lingolinks.biz

Congratulations

Well done....

Yes, it's time to celebrate, crack open the bubbly, eat some amazing cake or whatever floats your boat. You have now learned over 400 words of Bahasa Malaysia.

Using this style of learning is not only fun and speeds up the process of learning, but it's longer lasting too.

Now you have enough vocabulary to have a really great time anywhere in Malaysia, get a room, bargain at the market, order food, make friends and much more.

This learning style leads you in the direction of the words you are learning very quickly. It doesn't take long before the association you used disappears and the words you need are immediately available for you to speak and write.

The method is very effective and with a little practice, you will seat the words in your memory for life.

Now, go out there and ...

HAVE FUN with LINGO LINKS!

Lingo Links™ Language Learning
www.lingolinks.biz

About the Author

Born in 1963 in Leigh-on-sea, Essex, England, James was always a seeker, loving life and people. James education was marred with difficult teachers and, being shy, found languages a struggle so soon abandoned all hope of ever being able to converse in anything but English.

Educated to Degree level in computer science, James had a thirst to go beyond his seeming limitations. A job in IT Pre-Sales found James needing to quickly pick up communication and presentation skills and redundancy in 1991 gave him the opportunity to travel and further expand his horizons.

In 1992 James started to open more and more to connection, he discovered a wonderful dance form called Biodanza and went on to manage a holistic holiday centre in Greece.

Each year that followed led to a richer and richer life experience learning Pilates and the Guitar, becoming a Biodanza facilitator and Improvised Comedy teacher.

Since 2009, James has been looking after his parents in England and travelling in Asia, teaching and enjoying the culture and, whenever he can, writing in Bali. James captured, in this book, the method he finally used to overcome his younger learning difficulties. A combination of Comedy improv skill, an understanding of learning difficulties and a deep desire to share, gave birth to his remarkable books.

Connect with James

I really hope you got as much enjoyment out of learning Malaysian as I have. Please send me your comments. Your feedback will help me improve this learning series as it develops.

Email
james@lingolinks.biz

Web Site
www.lingolinks.biz

Twitter
https://twitter.com/EasyMalaysian

Facebook
http://www.facebook.com/lingolinks.biz

Amazon Author Page
http://www.amazon.co.uk/James-S-Harvey/e/B00I2P190K

Look out for the Lingo Links Apps on Google Play.

- Games to aid Learning
- Two way search
- Flick Learning ©
- Word review and more

Coming soon...

Answers to sections & quizzes

Here are the answers to help you check your translations.

There's often more than one way of saying something – you can double check online with many translation services –they are often not perfect – but will give you a pretty good idea.

Remember – simple is often more effective than complicated!

Past, Present, Future practice

Translate from	Answer
I will go to the beach	Saya akan pergi ke pantai
I've been swimming	Saya sudah selesai renang
I will eat later	Saya akan makan nanti
I went to the Airport yesterday	Semalam saya ke bandara
Saya mahu pergi ke Bandara esok	I want to go to the Airport tomorrow
Awak sudah makan?	Have you eaten?
Esok kamu akan pergi?	Will you go tomorrow?

Numbers check

Number	Translate this	Your Answer
24	Twenty four	Dua puluh empat
19	Nineteen	Sembilan-belas
5	Five	Lima
n/a	Twice	Dua kali
132	One hundred and thirty two	Satu ratus tiga puluh dua
2,000,000	Two Million	Dua Juta
7,000	Seven Thousand	Tujuh ribu
926	Nine hundred and twenty six	Sembilan ratus dua puluh enam
81	Eighty one	Lapan puluh satu

Sentence practice 1

Translate this	Answer
Where is the doctors	Di mana doktor
I want a bottle of water	Saya mahu sebotol air *
Yesterday I went for a swim	Semalam saya pergi berenang
I'd like some ice cream	Saya mahu ais krim
I'd like a young coconut please	Tolong saya mahu kelapa muda
Can I eat this	Boleh saya makan ini
What is this called	Apa ini namanya
I'm staying in the big house	Saya tinggal di rumah besar
Who's that?	Siapa Itu?
When did you wake up	Bila kamu bangun
Good evening, how's it going	Selamat petang, mahu ke mana

* Remember **se** means **one** of something.

Sentence practice 2

Translate this	Your Answer
Stop here please	Tolong berhenti di sini
I want to rent a room/house	Saya mahu sewa kamar/rumah
I feel ill	Saya rasa sakit
Where is a good place to eat?	Di mana tempat yang baik untuk makan?
Sorry, I don't understand	Maaf, saya tidak faham
No peanuts please, I'm allergic	Tolong tanpa kacang, saya alahan.
Excuse me, I need a fork	Maaf, saya perlu garpu
Where is the market?	Di mana pasar?
Where can I find an ATM?	Di mana ATM?
That was delicious	Itu enak
Is it safe here?	Apakah selamat di sini?
How much to go to the Airport?	Berapa harganya untuk pergi ke bandara?

Sentence practice 3

Translate this	Your Answer
Is this the road to Kuala Lumpur?	Apakah ini jalan ke Kuala Lumpur?
This is my friend John	Ini rakan saya John
I want a quiet room	Saya mahu rumah yang tenang
Look into my eyes	Lihat ke mataku
Are you married?	Apakah anda sudah berkahwin?
Is it far to the shops?	Apakah jauh ke kedai-kedia*
Please massage my feet	Tolong urut kaki saya
I have two older sisters	Saya ada dua kakak saudara perempuan
That's cool	Itu sempoi
I saw a film tonight	Saya tengok filem malam ini
Want to go dancing later?	Mahu pergi menari nanti?

* Remember you can repeat most nouns to make them plural.

Sentence practice 4

Translate this	Your Answer
I just got back from the village	Saya baru saja datang dari kampung
It was only twenty thousand Rupiah yesterday!	Itu cuma dua puluh ribu Rupiah semalam!
I would love to meet your family	Saya akan bahagia untuk bertemu keluarga awak
I will meet you at 5:30pm	Saya akan bertemu kamu pukul lima setengah siang ini
I'm looking for a house for 4 thousand a month or less	Saya cari rumah untuk empat ribu per bulan atau lebih murah
Yes, turn left by the big tree	Ya, belok kiri dekat pokok besar
What are you doing right now?	Apa yang awak lakukan sekarang?
I want to move out on January 2nd	Saya mahu pindah dua Januari
This is my second stay in Penang	Ini kedua kalinya saya tinggal di Penang

Pronunciation

The following guide will give you a great basis for how to pronounce words from their spelling. Unlike English, Malaysian is relatively consistent in matching sounds to spellings. There are some exceptions to this, and there are several sounds that can be tricky for English speakers. The important thing is to give it a go.

Vowels

Vowel and example	Used in Malaysian
a like *a* in *father*	datang, nama
e like *u* in *burn*	beli, semua
e between the *e* in *let* and the *a* in *late*	sekolah, seksi
i like *ee* in *feet*	pagi, kopi
o in olive	kopi, orang
u like *oo* in *mood*	buku, duduk**
ai like *ie* in *tie*	baik, sampai***
au like *ow* in *how*	mahu, saudara****

Note: There is no rule to know which way to pronounce *e* in a particular word without hearing it first - you can check an online service for the pronunciation (if you're not near a Malaysian).

**the *u* in the second syllable of *duduk* sounds more like the *oo* in *book*)

***the *ai* in *sampai* is often pronounced *ay* as in *day,* especially in Java

****the *au* in *saudara* is often pronounced *oe* as in *toe*)

In cases where two vowels are not separated by a consonant, just put the two vowel sounds together: siapa = *si apa*, etc. When a vowel is repeated, put a **glottal stop** (i.e. the catch in your throat when you say "uh-oh!") between the vowels: <u>maaf</u> = *ma-af*.

Consonants:

I. Consonants pronounced similar to English:

Consonant	Used in Malaysian
b as in *bed*	<u>b</u>ahasa, <u>s</u>ebelum
d as in *dad*	<u>d</u>uduk, <u>s</u>audara
f as in *feel*	<u>f</u>oto, <u>m</u>a-af
g as in *good*	<u>g</u>uru, <u>p</u>agi **Never as in giant**
l as in lap	<u>l</u>agi, <u>s</u>elamat
m as in *man*	<u>m</u>alam, <u>s</u>elamat
n as in *nap*	<u>N</u>anti, <u>t</u>ahun **ALSO SEE *ng, ny*, below**
s as in *see*	<u>s</u>iang, <u>k</u>elas **Never as in *boys***
w as in *well*	<u>b</u>awa, <u>s</u>ewa **Never as in *where***
y as in *yell*	<u>y</u>ang

II. Consonants pronounced differently than in English:

Consonants	Malaysian
j like the *j* in *Job*	<u>j</u>umpa, <u>s</u>ejuk
k like the *k* in *skate*	<u>k</u>opi, <u>a</u>is krim*
p like the *p* in *spot*	<u>p</u>agi, <u>a</u>pa*
t like the *t* in *stop*	<u>a</u>tas, <u>i</u>tu*

k, p, and t DO NOT have the puff of air they have in such English words as kill, put, and tap.

**NOTE: When k comes at the end of a word, the sound is cut off sharply (like the glottal stop mentioned above): baik, becak.

Lingo Links™ Language Learning
www.lingolinks.biz

ng like the *ng* in *singer*	tengah, datang

**NOTE: ng alone does not have the "hard" g, as in finger, which is always written as ngg in Malaysian: tinggal, penggaris

ny like the *ny* in *canyon*	banyak, nyamuk

III. Consonants that need special attention:

Consonant	Used in Malaysian
c like *c* in *cello* or the *ch* in *chat*, <u>Never like the c in cat</u>	cinta, kucing
h as in *house*, but it can also appear at the end of words:	hari, bahasa, sekolah
r like the *tt* in *butter*. It is usually a tap of the tongue behind the teeth, though it sometimes is more of a trill (like the *rr* in Spanish *arriba*, especially at the ends of words	rumah, saudara, khabar

The letters *q, v, x, z* are very rare in Malaysian, and are mostly found in words borrowed from English, Dutch or Arabic.

q similar to English *k*	Qur'an
v similar to English *v* or *f*	veto, vitri
x like English *x*	xerox
z like English *z* or *j*	zebra

Alphabet

Here is how you pronounce the alphabet in Malaysian:

a ehy	b bee	c see	d dee	e ee	f ef	g gee
h hech	i ai	j jay	k keh	l el	m em	n en
o oh	p pee	q que	r ar	s es	t tee	u yu
v vee	w doble yu	x eks	y wai	z zed		

Baahasa Malaysia

Index

About - Mengenai 77
Above - Atas................86
After - Selepas.............71
Afternoon - Tengah hari..56
Again - Lagi.................97
Ago - Masa lalu.............73
Airport - Bandara 28
All - Semua 65
Allergy/Allergic - Alahan 101
Alone - Sendiri.............38
Already - Sudah 29
Also - Juga..................42
April - April............... 113
At - Di......................85
ATM - ATM 70
August - Ogos 113
Bad - Buruk.................93
Bag - Beg 49
Bank - Bank.................89
Bath/Bathe - Mandi 50
Be my guest - Silahkan....28
Beach - Pantai. 29
Beautiful - Cantik 92
Bed - Katil 73
Before - Sebelum..........85
Besides - Selain............76
Best - Terbaik..............88
Big - Besar 33
Birthday - Hari Lahir 52
Black - Hitam...............97
Blue - Biru 41
Book - Buku 22
Bottle - Botol...............38
Boyfriend - Teman lelaki .93
Bring - Bawa................39
Broken - Rosak............86

Brother - Saudara laki-laki
.... 86
Brown - Coklat 30
Build - Buat 74
Bus - Bas.................... 65
Buy - Beli 34
Cake - Kek 88
Can - Boleh 23
Car - Kereta................ 28
Cat - Kucing............... 32
Chair - Kerusi.............. 53
Change - Ubah............101
Cheap - Murah............. 68
Children - Kanak-kanak .101
Class - Kelas 43
Clever - Pandai............ 64
Clock - Jam 119
Close(d) - Tutup 96
Clothes - Pakaian 39
Coconut - Kelapa 32
Coffee - Kopi 85
Cold - Sejuk...............117
Cold (virus) - Selsema 49
Come - Datang............. 85
Come along (Join) - Ikut . 52
Cook - Masak.............. 53
Cool - Sempoi.............. 92
Credit for phone - Top up 73
Dance - Tarian 64
Darling - Sayang........... 92
Date -Tanggal.............114
Day - Hari 86
December - Disember ...113
Delicious - Sedap 71
Dentist - Doktor gigi 88
Different - Berbeza 77

Difficult – Sukar 88
Dinner – Makan Malam 93
Do – Lakukan............... 101
Doctor - Dokter 42
Don't – Jangan 53
Download – Muat turun ... 77
Drink - Minum 33
Driver – Pemandu......... 65
Dry – Kering............... 74
Eat - Makan 33
Eight - Lapan 104
Electricity – Listrik 89
Eleven – Sebelas 106
Emotion – Emosi 76
Evening – Petang.......... 56
Ever – Pernah.............. 83
Every - Setiap 65
Everywhere – Di mana-mana
.... 71
Exit – Keluar 76
Expense – Belanja 42
Expensive – Mahal 88
Eyes – Mata................ 92
Family – Keluarga........ 101
Fan – Kipas 70
Far – Jauh 89
Fast – Cepat (cepat)....... 70
Fat – Gemuk 86
Father – Bapa.............. 96
Favourite – Kegemaran ... 71
February - Februari......113
Feel – Rasa 53
Feet – Kaki 96
Film – Filem................ 93
Find – Cari.................. 64
Finished - Selasai 22
Fire – Api 76
First – Pertama 110
First/Before – Dahulu 91

Five - Lima 104
Fix – Membaiki 96
Flower(s) – bunga (bunga) 70
Foot – Kaki...................96
Forest – hutan 67
Fork - Garpu 38
Four - Empat 104
Friday - Jumaat 115
Friend - Rakan 89
From – Dari 53
Fruit – Buah-(buah). 41
Girlfriend – Teman wanita 92
Give – Beri. 39
Glass (of water) – gelas ...49
Go – Pergi 19
Go out – Ke luar...........76
Goodbye – Selamat Jalan 56, 57
Goodbye – Selamat tinggal
.... 56, 57
Goodwill – Selamat........55
Hair - Rambut 38
Half – Separuh 38
Hands – Tangan 96
Happy - Bahagia 85
Head – Kepala..............65
Hello/Hi - Halo/Hai.........10
Help (assist) – Bantuan 76
Holiday – Cuti 93
Hot - Panas 41
Hour – Jam................ 119
House – Rumah 28
How – Bagaimana..........22
How are you - Apa kabar . 19
How long - Berapa lama ..71
How many - Berapa........23
How much – Berapa banyak
............................23
Hug – Pelukan 92

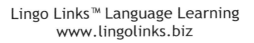

Lingo Links™ Language Learning
www.lingolinks.biz

Hundred – Ratus 108
Husband – Suami 93
I – Saya 18
Ice Cream – Ais krim 52
If – Jika 41
In – Di 85
In the process of – Sedang 36
Indeed – Benar 97
Inside – Dalam 100
Isn't it – Kan 48
January – Januari 113
Jar – Jar 77
Jug – Jag 97
July – Julai 113
June – Jun 113
Just now – Sebentar tadi . 65
Knife – Pisau 38
Know – Tahu 29
Lamp – Lampu 49
Language – Bahasa 10
Late – Lambat 64
Later – Kemudian 41
Later – Nanti 32
Learn(ing) – Belajar 28
Left – Kiri 85
Legs – Kaki 96
Letter – Surat 100
Light – Lampu 49
Like – Suka 71
Listen – Dengar 77
Look – Melihat 64
Look for – Cari 64
Loose change – Wang kecil
.... 100
Love – Cinta 92
Make – Buat 74
Man – Lelaki 100
Many – Banyak 42
March – Mac 113

Market – Pasar 42
Married – Berkahwin 93
Massage – Urut 53
May – Mei 113
Me – Saya 18
Meat – Daging 48
Meet – Bertemu 64
Milk – Susu 67
Million – Juta 42
Minute – Minit 119
Mobile Phone – Telephon
bimbit 88
Monday – Isnin 115
Money – Wang/Duit 73
Month – Bulan 67
More – Lebih 39
Morning – Pagi 55
Mosquito – Nyamuk 70
Mother – Emak/Mak 86
Motor Bike – Motosikal 33
Move in – Pindah 41
Move out – Pindah 41
Must – Mesti 74
My – Saya 18
Name – Nama 18
Near – Dekat 65
Need – Perlu 74
Never – Tidak pernah 83
New – Baru 96
Newspaper – Surat khabar
.... 100
Night – Malam 56
Nine – Sembilan 104
No –Tidak 18
Not – bukan 48
Not –Tidak 18
Not yet – Belum 65
November – November .. 113
Now – Sekarang 34

O'clock– Pukul.............118
October - Oktober.......113
Often - Sering 71
OK, Fine - Baik 22
Old – Tua 88
Older sibling – Kakak.....96
Olive – Zaitun..............77
On – Atas 86
On - Di 85
One – Satu.................104
Only – Hanya/Cuma........74
Open – Buka................68
Orange (Colour) – Jingga . 73
Orange (Fruit) – Oren 71
Ordinary – Biasa............74
Originate - Berasal 74
Pain - Sakit..................71
Pancake – Penkek.........88
Party - Pesta...............64
Peanut – Kacang............70
Pen - Pena. 39
People – Orang 67
Person– Orang 67
Photo(graph) – foto........52
Pineapple - Nanas 52
Place - Tempat.............73
Plan – Rancangan 76
Plastic – Plastik............49
Plate – Pinggan 49
Please - Tolong............19
Police – Polis..............97
Price – Harga(nya) 19
Problem - Masalah.........29
Quiet (Calm) – Tenang....88
Rain – Hujan 70
Rarely – Jarang.............77
Read – Baca 52
Ready (get ready) - Bersedia
...........................76

Red – Merah 33
Religion – Agama 77
Rent – Sewa 68
Repair – Membaiki..........96
Restaurant – Restoran.....32
Return - Pulang............38
Rice - Nasi 28
Rice Field – Sawah 101
Right – Kanan..............65
River – Sungai 67
Road – Jalan................50
Rubbish – Sampah.........73
Safe – Selamat 76, 78
Salad - Salad...............53
Same - Sama...............42
Sand - Pasir................67
Saturday - Sabtu.........115
Sauce – Sos 68
School – Sekolah...........97
Season - Musim 117
Second - Saat 119
See - Melihat...............64
September - September 113
Seven - Tujuh 104
Sexy – Seksi................92
Shoes – Kasut..............74
Shop – Kedai...............68
Sick - Sakit..................71
Sister – Saudara perempuan
...........................89
Sit - Duduk..................48
Six - Enam 104
Skirt - Skirt.................39
Sleep – Tidur 73
Small – Kecil.............. 100
Smell – Bau 97
So - Jadi.................... 100
Something - Sesuatu.......77

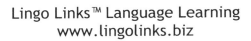

Sometimes - Kadang-Kadang
................................68
Sorry - Ma-af 70
Spicy - Pedas 85
Spoon - Sudu 49
Start - Bermula 76
Stay - Tinggal 23
Still - Masih 41
Stomach - Perut 97
Stop - Berhenti 50
Straight on - Lurus 97
Strike - Pukul 118
Study - Belajar..............28
Sugar - Gula 32
Sun - Matahari 64
Sunday - Ahad 115
Sure - Pasti 86
Sweet - Manis 89
Swimming - Renang........29
Table - Meja.................67
Take - Ambil. 39
Take care - Jaga diri 86
Tall - Tinggi................ 101
Taste - Rasa 53
Taxi - Teksi..................73
Tea - Teh 33
Teacher - Guru 53
Television - Televisyen ...53
Ten - Sepuluh............. 104
Thank you - Terima kasih 18
That - Itu.....................23
Then - Kemudian...........41
There - Di sana 32
There is/are - Ada 29
They - Mereka 39
Thirsty - Haus...............38
This - Ini 85
Thousand - Ribu 108
Three - Tiga 104

Thursday - Khamis........115
Time - Kali 110
To - Ke 18
Toilet - Tandas 32
Tomorrow - Esok 29
Towel - Tuala.............. 96
Tree - Pokok............... 100
True - Benar 97
Try - Cuba................. 71
Tuesday - Selasa 115
Turn - Belok 101
Turn (Switch) off - Tutup 49
Turn (Switch) on - Hidupkan
.... 67
Two - Dua 104
Under - Bawah 101
Understand - Faham 19
Until - Sehingga 85
Upstairs - Di atas........... 86
Usual - Biasa 74
Vegetables - Sayur 39
Vegetarian - Vegetarian.. 48
Very - Sangat 52
Village - Kampung 41
Wake up - Bangun 39
Walk - Jalan-jalan 93
Want - Mahu 22
Watch - Tengok 93
Watch (wrist) - Jam 119
Water - Air 29
Weather - Cuaca 68
Wednesday - Rabu........115
Week - Minggu.............. 42
Wet - Basah 88
What - Apa 49
When - Bila 33
Where - Di Mana 22
Where to - Ke mana....... 30
Which - Yang 52

White - Putih 67
Who - Siapa 23
Wife – Isteri 93
Will – Akan 28
Without - Tanpa 33
Woman – Wanita 89
Word - Perkataan 48
Work – Kerja 68
Worry – Khuatir 97

Write - Tulis 68
Year – Tahun 52
Yellow – Kuning 74
Yes - Ya 10
Yesterday – Semalam 33
You – Awak 22
Young – Muda 42
Younger sibling – Adik ... 100
Your – Awak 22

Your Notes.

Notes.

Notes.

Notes.

Notes.

Printed in Great Britain
by Amazon